TRIUMPH OF THE LAMB

A Self-Study Guide
to the Book of Revelation

TED GRIMSRUD
Foreword by Willard M. Swartley

HERALD PRESS
Scottdale, Pennsylvania
Kitchener, Ontario
1987

Library of Congress Cataloging-in-Publication Data

Grimsrud, Ted, 1954—
  Triumph of the lamb.

  Bibliography: p.
  Includes index.
  1. Bible. N.T. Revelation—Study. 2. Bible. N.T.
Revelation—Criticism, interpretation, etc. I. Title.
BS2825.5.G75 1987   228'.0076   87-409
ISBN 0-8361-3438-9 (pbk.)

TRIUMPH OF THE LAMB
Copyright © 1987 by Herald Press, Scottdale, Pa. 15683-1999
     Published simultaneously in Canada by Herald Press,
     Kitchener, Ont. N2G 4M5. All rights reserved.
Library of Congress Catalog Card Number: 87-409
International Standard Book Number: 0-8361-3438-9
Printed in the United States of America
Design by Gwen M. Stamm

87 88 89 90 91 92 93 10 9 8 7 6 5 4 3 2 1

TRIUMPH
OF THE
LAMB

Dedicated
to the memory of
my father
Carl M. Grimsrud, Jr.
(1917-1984)

Contents

Foreword

Revelation has been the least used book in the Bible by most Christians and at the same time the most misused book by some Christians. On numerous occasions when I have led Bible studies on Revelation in congregational settings, I have received comments such as, "Until now I have never studied Revelation because I was afraid of it. Thanks for helping me understand it and leading me to hear it as a powerful call to worship God."

The central issue in Revelation is, Whom do you worship? Set within the context of persecution and martyrdom, the question cuts into us with a razor-sharp political edge. Our loyalty to Jesus Christ, our willingness to suffer, and our faithful endurance are all tested. But the swelling of the choirs of praise empower us to hold steadfast—to see the kingdoms of the world become the kingdom of our Lord's Christ and to sing, "Alleluia! The Lord God Almighty reigns!"

I heartily recommend this study for our churches for these reasons. First, it combines brief but helpful commentary on the text with reflection upon the issues of faithfulness in our time. In this respect it captures the Word of God in Revelation for us today.

Second, it is designed well for group study in the churches.

Each chapter begins with study questions and each ends with provocative questions for group discussion. The meditation in each chapter creates the right mood for in-depth grappling with the significance of that Scripture.

Third, Grimsrud avoids the speculative pitfalls of the more popular treatments of Revelation. His perception of the symbolic and theological depth of Revelation is commendable. With Jacques Ellul he sees the sinister depth of evil and its beastly expressions then and now. *But* he sees also the ultimacy of God's justice, goodness, and love.

This is a book for which to be grateful. I hope and pray that many people in our churches will use it and thus exchange the often misplaced questions about Revelation with a new vision of

> steadfast trust,
> the slain Lamb,
> and worship of God!

"For the testimony of Jesus is the spirit of prophecy" (19:10d). Together may we conquer. Together may we sing around the throne:

> Worthy is the Lamb, who was slain,
> to receive power,
> wealth and wisdom,
> might and honor,
> glory and blessing!

—*Willard M. Swartley*
Associated Mennonite Biblical Seminaries

Author's Preface

This is a book about the active Bible study of a particular text, the book of Revelation. I use the term active Bible study in two senses. The first sense has to do with our need to approach the Bible *actively*—asking questions and seeking answers. To facilitate this process I have included study questions at the beginning of each section which are intended to help you to ask questions of the biblical text as you are reading it. The second sense has to do with our need to actively apply what we learn from Bible study to our lives. I have thus included some application-oriented mediations in each section and have concluded each section with questions for thought and discussion.

My basic approach fits under the general rubric of "inductive" Bible study. According to one explanation of biblical interpretation,° the inductive method involves paying careful attention to both the literary structure and context of a passage; looking at words, sentences, paragraphs, and larger blocks of material; and asking questions such as who? what? where? when? and why? It notes re-

---

° *Biblical Interpretation in the Life of the Church* (Scottdale, Pa.: Mennonite Publishing House, 1977).

curring themes, causes and effects, and relationships within the passage, as well as similarities to and differences from other passages of the Bible. The goal of the inductive method is to allow our conclusions to grow out of the text.

This explanation lists nine steps to the process:

1. *Observe carefully what the text says.* To understand the text itself, we need to look at it closely. Bible study means studying the *Bible.* This point is the particular concern of my study questions. Most of the questions are meant to facilitate a close reading of the text. I recommend that you read through the entire passage first and then go back over it with the questions in hand. The answers to most of them should be apparent as you read and reflect. A few might require looking at a Bible atlas or Bible dictionary or encyclopedia. Do not take the questions too seriously. They are meant only to be an aid for *you* to understand Revelation. If you are studying this book in a small group, utilize your communal resources. The more time spent with prediscussion reading and reflecting on the text in the light of the study questions, the better suited the group will be to go on from there and work together at interpreting the significance of the passage you are studying.

2. *Be sensitive to different literary forms.* The Bible is made up of various literary forms, including narrative, parable, poetry, and discourse. These must be taken into account and interpreted accordingly.

3. *Study the historical and cultural contexts of the passage.* A study of the Bible is always a study of a people. It is necessary therefore to enter the world of the Hebrew people and the people of the early church. This includes understanding their ways of thinking, their cultural pattern, and their distinctiveness amid the surrounding cultures and nations.

4. *Make wise use of various translations.* A comparison of alternate renderings of a passage may lead to a clearer understanding of the biblical text.

5. *Consider how the text has been interpreted by others.* Bible commentaries and Bible dictionaries can be valuable resources. I have included a list of books I have found helpful in studying Revelation at the back of this book.

6. *Consider the message of the Bible as a whole.* It is necessary

to take seriously the message of the Bible as a whole and compare Scripture with Scripture.

7. *Meditate upon the Word in the spirit of prayer.* We should reflect on what we are learning, asking God to open our eyes to deeper insights and the power to make these a part of how we live.

8. *Listen for the guidance of the Spirit, individually and congregationally.* The experience of the Spirit, the interpretation of the Word, and the understanding of the church should agree.

9. *Respond obediently to the Bible's message.* The Bible speaks to us only if we are open to its message. Through faithful responses to the Word, we discover the power of the biblical message to upbuild the interpreting community.

While I accept the basic validity of the inductive method, I think that several potential problems with it should also be kept in mind. For one thing, it can seem burdensome and complicated. My assumption is that learning from the Bible should not be an overly complicated task. Certainly, the harder we work at it and the more resources we can bring to bear on our learning, the better off we will be. And portions of the Bible like the book of Revelation are at times quite obscure. But we should not think that we must always follow every step of the inductive method in order to benefit from Bible study. The best resource is a relative simple one: a small group of sincere, openhearted people attending to the Word of God together.

A second potential problem is that the inductive method can lead us to assume that it is necessary, or even possible, to approach the biblical text strictly on its own terms. Our goal is certainly that of hearing the text itself. But we cannot, and should not attempt to, separate ourselves from our own concerns and beliefs. Our reason for reading the Bible is to gain insight for living faithfully today. The inductive method can assist us in hearing the message of the Bible, but it does so only as we are asking the Bible *our* questions and filtering what we hear through *our* ears.

The third potential problem is that we see the process of Bible study as *first* studying the Bible and *then* applying it to life. Actually, both need to happen simultaneously. It is only in the context of attempting to practice obedience to Jesus that we can formulate authentic questions which can truly get at what the Bible is about. Yet it is only through an understanding of biblical teaching that we can know what obedience to Jesus looks like. Action and study go together.

With these qualifications, I would endorse the inductive method as an invaluable approach to hearing what God has to say to us through Scripture.

My own exposure to the inductive method as applied to the book of Revelation dates back to January 1981 when I took a class on Revelation from Gertrude Roten at the Associated Mennonite Biblical Seminaries. Professor Roten is my model of a teacher of the Bible. My memories of her masterful classroom presence and contagious enthusiasm remain vivid. She also provided the original form (which I have adapted) of the study questions which begin each section.

I would also like to acknowledge my indebtedness to Willard M. Swartley, Professor Roten's AMBS colleague who skillfully guided me through Biblical Hermeneutics and New Testament Theology and Ethics and whose book, *Mark: The Way for All Nations* (Herald Press, 1979) is an excellent example of the inductive method in practice. I have learned a great deal from Professors Roten and Swartley, but would emphasize that neither should be held responsible for my more "problematic" interpretations in this book.

The Eugene (Oreg.) Mennonite Church and Trinity Mennonite Church (Glendale, Ariz.) provided supportive environments for the initial presentation of much of this material. I continue in my heartfelt gratitude to each.

—Ted Grimsrud
Berkeley, California

TRIUMPH
OF THE
LAMB

And they sang a new song, saying,

> *Worthy art thou to take the scroll and to open its seals, for thou wast slain and by thy blood didst ransom persons for God from every tribe and tongue and people and nation, and hast made them a kingdom and priests to our God, and they shall reign on earth.*

Then I looked, and I heard around the throne and the living creatures and elders the voice of many angels, numbering myriads of myriads and thousands of thousands, saying with a loud voice,

> *Worthy is the Lamb who was slain, to receive power and wealth and wisdom and might and honor and glory and blessing!*

And I heard every creature in heaven and on earth and under the earth and in the sea, and all therein, saying,

> *To him who sits upon the throne and to the Lamb be blessing and honor and glory and might for ever and ever!*

And the four living creatures said, "Amen!" and the elders fell down and worshiped (Rev. 5:9-14).

Introduction

The book of Revelation is one of the strangest books in the Bible and in many ways one of the hardest to understand. At the same time, perhaps because of its difficulty, Revelation has led to a large number of speculative writings and has been utilized by many people to support many different views of God, Jesus, and the future.

My hope in writing this short book is to aid interested people in understanding Revelation a bit better. I doubt very much whether anyone can honestly say that he or she fully understands it. But I am convinced that Revelation is to a large degree understandable, and that as we understand it better, John's words, "Blessed is he who reads aloud the words of the prophecy, and blessed are those who hear, and who keep what is written therein," (1:3) will be true for us.

Approaches to Revelation

How we understand Revelation depends a lot on how we approach it. If we expect to find predictions about the future that might come true at any time, then we will look for those. If we expect to see a veiled condemnation of the Roman Empire, we will look for that. To a certain degree, these are choices we make before we begin to study Revelation. But hopefully, we can remain open to the evidence as we go along and let the actual content of the book lead us in our understanding.

Over the past two thousand years, four distinct approaches have emerged concerning Revelation, though more and more scholars combine one or more.

The first, called the "preterist" view, sees the events recorded in Revelation as relating strictly to the time in which they were recorded. The visions had immediate relevance and were not intended to predict the far-off future. In particular, this view takes the Roman Empire and the early church's struggle to survive in the face of Roman persecution as the main concern. The main focus of the study of Revelation then becomes seeking to understand what the book meant then. Perhaps some present-day applications can be drawn, but they are secondary.

The second approach, the "historicist," sees Revelation as a history of the church. It contains some information concerning just about every age of the church, including some about the future. The letters to the seven churches are especially used in this way. They are interpreted as seven stages of church history, from the time of the early church to the end of time.

The third approach, the "idealist" or philosophy-of-history approach, sees Revelation primarily in symbolic terms. In this view, Revelation expresses a timeless philosophy of history in which God's people struggle with evil until God eventually destroys evil and establishes the kingdom. The visions are symbolic of the spiritual struggle between good and evil—not literal.

The fourth approach, the "futurist," sees Revelation as portraying the future—not just for John's time, but for our time too. Most people taking this approach find in the visions enough clues to make them believe that the events pictured in Revelation are soon to take place. The future pictured here is soon to become present.

Most contempoary scholars combine either the preterist and idealist views or the preterist and futurist views.

My Perspective

I first became aware of the book of Revelation when I was told early in my Christian life that Revelation contained predictions which were being fulfilled or were soon to be fulfilled. I did not study the book as such. My acquaintance with it was limited to isolated verses that were used in discussions about how we were in the end times and how the great tribulation, the rapture, Armageddon, and antichrist were all just around the corner. This came from sermons in my church, listening to tapes by Dallas Seminary professors and evangelist Jack Van Impe, and reading books by popular writers Hal Lindsey and Salem Kirban. Reading Revelation itself was just too confusing.

As I began to read more, I learned that this school of thought was not accepted by everyone. I read some critiques that convinced me to change my views, but I still did not understand what Revelation was about. I was motivated to begin to work at understanding Revelation by some arguments I had with a friend about pacifism. He said that we should not be pacifists because God is not a pacifist; God fights wars in the Old Testament and in Revelation. So I decided to see if he was right.

I began to read various commentaries and other books on Revelation and became fascinated with the book as a whole. I discovered that there has been a good deal of serious scholarship done on Revelation. I was surprised at the commonality of general conclusions.

The kinds of conclusions I have come to and the applications I have drawn have been affected greatly by the kinds of concerns that I have had. After giving up on Hal Lindsey's approach to the Bible, I became much less concerned with futuristic predictions. I started being more interested in what Revelation says about how we should live *now* and how this affects how we should look at our world *now*. Social concerns like war and peace and economics have become more central to me, and I have wanted to know how the Bible, including Revelation, relates to those concerns. My view of "prophecy" changed from seeing it primarily in terms of predictions of the future to seeing it in terms of proclaiming God's truth for today. I now see prophecy more as forthtelling than foretelling.

At the same time, I have wanted to be sensitive to Revelation's message on its own terms. Why was it originally written? Who was it written to? What was their situation? What were their needs? How does the book address those needs? In answering these questions, I hope to get insights into my questions for the modern world.

I recognize that the questions of Revelation's first readers were not exactly the same as mine today. Therefore some translating is necessary. It is dangerous to ignore the barriers created by two thousand years and different languages and cultures. Revelation was not originally written for twentieth-century Americans. To get its point, we need to respect and take into account its original setting.

Recognizing the need to respect the original setting of Revelation, I would to a large degree take a preterist approach to interpreting it. And then, on the basis of my understanding of what it meant *then*, I would understand its message largely in terms of the idealist approach. In my view, the visions and imagery of Revelation symbolize God's work in human history, God's victory over evil in Jesus' work, and God's moving history toward its consummation in the ultimate destruction of evil and the establishment of the New Jerusalem.

I have found Revelation extremely interesting and relevant to my thinking about our world today. These are a few of the applications that I would draw from the message of the book:

(1) No matter how bleak things look in the present, God is in ultimate control of things and is working things out for the good. Therefore we can have hope.

(2) It is self-destructive to retaliate with evil against evil. If we do so, we become evil ourselves and lose God's spiritual protection.

(3) That the world is hopelessly chaotic and that evil is in control is the superficial view. The "revelation" helps us to see that what is really going on is that God is facilitating evil's self-destruction.

(4) Suffering can be redemptive if we remain faithful to God.

(5) The most powerful thing in the universe is Christ's suffering love, seen especially in the cross, not the might of kings on earth. Imitating Christ's suffering love is how we can be victorious.

(6) There is continuity between this world and the next. The good things that we do—not just moral obedience but also human creativity—will be part of the New Jerusalem.

Revelation and Apocalyptic Literature

The Greek word for "revelation" that is used in 1:1 is *apokalypsis* (apocalypse). This word, when used elsewhere in the New Testament, refers to the supernatural revealing of truths from

God that are previously unknown to people and could not be discovered by people on their own (cf. Rom. 16:25 and Gal. 1:12). The "revelation" comes from outside; it comes from God. So John, when he says this book is an apocalypse, is making high claims.

The use of this word also places Revelation in a category of other ancient works now known as apocalyptic literature. This includes the book of Daniel from the Old Testament and such Jewish and Christian extrabiblical writings as the Book of Enoch, the Apocalypse of Baruch, the Apocalypse of Paul, and the Apocalypse of Peter.

The general characteristics of apocalyptic literature include the extensive use of symbolism; use of the vision as a major instrument of revelation; concentration on the close of this age and the dramatic inauguration of the age to come; the unveiling of the spiritual order lying behind and determining the course of events in history; the use of common motifs (e.g., dragon and lion); and a certain dualism— between this age and the next, good and evil, black and white.

The book of Revelation, however, has some unique characteristics compared to most of the other apocalypses:

(1) It does not claim to be written by someone other than the true author. Most of the others claim to be written by some earlier, well-known person, like Moses, Enoch, Paul, or Peter. The author of Revelation identifies himself only as a prophet and pastor. If he is John the apostle he does not play up that identity—something which would surely have happened were the book pseudepigraphical.

(2) The date and place of origin are clear.

(3) Generally in apocalyptic literature all history is directed toward a future end. In Revelation the key event has *already* happened in the life, death, and resurrection of Jesus.

(4) The dualism of good and evil is limited. Revelation proclaims the absolute lordship of God. Evil is already decisively defeated.

(5) Revelation identifies itself as prophecy, thus self-consciously tying itself with the Old Testament prophets, not the Jewish apocalypticists. The book is the Revelation of Jesus Christ, not the Revelation of John or of any other writer.

Given these significant differences, it seems to me important to distance Revelation a bit from apocalyptic literature in general. We should respect the book's self-identification as a "prophecy" (1:3; 22:7; 22:10; 22:18; 22:19).

The first writing prophets in the Old Testament lived in the eighth century B.C. Their ministry has been summarized by Bernhard W. Anderson in his book *The Eighth Century Prophets* (Philadelphia: Fortress, 1978):

> The proper place to begin to understand the prophetic proclamation is with their sense of time, and particularly their awareness of the relation of the future to the present. The eighth century prophets perceived that a storm was coming—"the east wind of Yahweh . . . rising from the wilderness," as Hosea said (Hos. 13:15). As messengers of God, their task was to make the eschatological shock of God's future effective in the present, so that Israel—the people of God—might recover their identity and their vocation and so that possibly, in the incalculable grace of God, there might be a transition from death to life. (p. 22)

The book of Revelation shares these characteristics to a large degree. John is presenting God's Word for the present of his readers by giving pictures of God's future. The message in Revelation is, "Hold fast to the faithfulness you are now living." But in many of the Old Testament prophets, it was, "Repent and change your ways."

However, the letters to the seven churches indicate that John was intending to communicate the latter as well. In any case, his method of communicating, like the ancient prophets, was "to make the eschatological shock of God's future effective in the present."

The prophet "forthtells" God's truth to the present, utilizing the God-given gift of discernment into the true realities of the present. What really matters is the truth of the prophet's vision of God's nature and will, and of the world in that light. To the degree that the prophet foretells the future, this is done in the service of speaking about God's will for the present. The prophets were not concerned with speaking of the future for its own sake.

Thus the book of Revelation focuses on the needs of John's readers in the face of their present-day reality. They needed encouragement to stand strong in the face of persecution from the Roman Empire and some of their Jewish opponents. Others needed exhortation to not mix the gospel with pagan religion, and especially not to become conformed to the world and to bow down to Caesar. In both cases, a revelation of the true nature of the secular order and its fate was needful. So also was a revelation of the power of God to judge and cleanse the world of all evil and bring about the promised new order. Revelation speaks of the future in order to speak effectively to the present.

The idea that Revelation contains visions of things which apply only to the far-off future and could not really have had any meaning to anyone prior to that future time, directly contradicts this understanding of prophecy.

Revelation speaks to us today to the degree that we *share* the situation of John's readers—to the degree that we need encouragement to stand strong in the face of evil and exhortation to not bend the knee to the gods of this world.

The Format of This Study

This book is intended to be a study guide to the book of Revelation. For those who wish to use it as such, I have a few suggestions. Revelation is a difficult book to understand by oneself, and is best suited to be studied with others. But even when working together, each of us must also work at it individually.

Read the book on your own. Read each section a few times on your own prior to looking at my interpretations and other resources. In reading the whole book or the different sections, take notes of your observations and questions. One way to do that is to read each section five times and to write down twenty observations and questions. This will help a good deal in knowing what to look for when you go on to look at what other people think.

I have included with each section a list of study questions. You may attempt to answer them during your observation process. They can also serve as aids when you read my discussion of the passages and look at other commentaries and study books.

The bulk of this book is a passage-by-passage interpretation followed by short essays discussing what I see as some of the main issues addressed by Revelation and how those issues apply to us today. At the back of the book, I have supplied a bibliography of books I have found most helpful in my study of Revelation.

Questions for Thought and Discussion

(1) Read the book of Revelation in its entirety, preferably at one sitting. Note questions you would like to pursue further.

(2) What seem to you to be the main themes of the book? Are they unique to this book in the New Testament? Are they central or peripheral to the gospel as you understand it?

(3) How would you characterize the mood of the book?

(4) Have you encountered Revelation in the past? If so, what did you think of it?

(5) Do you think that Revelation has something to say to Christians today? If so, what? If not, why not?

(6) How do you respond to people who see a blueprint for the future in Revelation? Those who see in it a justification, at least implicitly, for violence? Those who see it as sub-Christian?

(7) What do you know about the Roman Empire that would shed light on Revelation? Do you see any relevant parallels between Rome and the United States?

(8) What do you think John's social location (e.g., social class, economic status, racial and national identification) was? How does it compare to ours? Who today might be closest to John's social location (e.g., North American Mennonites, Brazilian peasant Catholics, Russian baptists)?

(9) How might John's social location affect his message? How much "translating" must we do to move from John's situation to ours?

Revelation One
Prologue

Study Questions

(1) How is the book characterized in 1:1-3?

(2) In what role is John cast?

(3) What is it that must soon take place?

(4) Who are the recipients of this letter (1:4, 11)? Why these churches?

(5) Why does John cast the Christian community in a priestly role (1:6)?

(6) Note how God is characterized in 1:8. Why should God be described this way?

(7) How is the author identified in 1:9? Where was Patmos located? What is the "testimony of Jesus"?

(8) What is the meaning of 1:10? How are the "seeing" and the "hearing" described in 1:10-11 to be understood?

(9) Note the elaborate imagery employed in 1:12-16. From what sources is it drawn? What is the meaning and function of the various images?

(10) What additional understandings of Christ are supplied by 1:17-20?

(11) What is the most important verse in this vision of Christ?

How may this verse influence one's interpretation of the entire book?

(12) What is the place and function of this vision in the larger structure and message of the book as you understand it?

1:1-3 Descriptive Introduction

These verses introduce and identify the book. They indicate what it is, where it came from, and what its intent is.

This book is called a "revelation of Jesus Christ" (1:1) and a prophecy (1:3). The Greek word for "revelation" is *apokalypsis*. The meaning of apocalypse and of prophecy was discussed above in the introduction. These verses indicate that John is self-consciously placing this book in those categories.

One of the main implications he draws from this is that this book speaks for God. John explicitly makes higher claims for the divine inspiration and authority of his book than any of the other New Testament writers for their books. According to John, this book's origins are with God, not with human intellect or wisdom.

The intent of the book is to bless those who hear and keep the prophecy it contains (1:3). John seeks to do this by showing his readers what must soon take place. It is important that John do so because "the time is near."

The expression "for the time is near" (1:3) was adapted from Daniel 2:28 ("in the latter days"). For the early church the latter days were now present with the coming of Jesus (cf. Acts 2:14-36 where Peter quoted Joel to say that the latter days have come). What must soon take place was the unfolding of the events of these latter days. This included especially the incoming of the Gentiles into God's people and the pouring out of the Holy Spirit and refers to everything from the time of John the Baptist to the end. It is doubtful that Paul or John expected that the latter days would last as long as they have—but years are human time, not God's time.

That the congregations were to "keep what is written" in this book (1:3) indicates that John was giving moral instruction to them, not esoteric knowledge or predictions about the far-distant future.

The one "who reads" this book (1:3) is most likely a reference to a person who would read the book aloud in the church, not to a private student. This book was meant for the church.

1:4-8 Salutation and Doxology

Verse 4 indicates that this book was meant to be seen as a letter from John to the "seven churches that are in Asia." The letter format is another indication that the intention of the book was pastoral and prophetic in the sense described above. It was addressed to specific people in a specific historical setting and was intended to address their needs.

John was writing to seven concrete, real-life churches. However, the fact that there were precisely seven indicates that the universal church was also meant to receive this message. More than seven churches existed in the area, so it was a conscious choice by John to single out only seven. The number seven is a significant symbolic number in Revelation, as it is throughout the Bible and in extrabiblical Jewish and Christian literature of the ancient world. The number seven in Revelation generally alludes to wholeness and completeness. So, while John is writing to seven specific churches, he is also writing to the whole church. His messages to the seven churches in chapters 2 and 3 show that he had pastoral concerns unique for each. Nevertheless, as a whole they communicate pastoral concerns that apply to any and all churches.

The "seven spirits" alluded to in verse 4 are probably a reference to the Holy Spirit, equally present in each church. In verse 5, Jesus Christ is given three titles. The first is "faithful witness." The term *faithful* is used in Revelation of people who give their lives for God's sake. *Witness* translates the Greek word *martus*, which is also translated as martyr. Jesus Christ was faithful unto death. This kind of faithfulness is the way that God overcomes evil. It serves as an encouragement to those of John's readers who might be facing the threat of martyrdom. They are following the path of Jesus—the one who went before them.

The second title here is "firstborn of the dead." This emphasizes his resurrection, his victory over death and evil. The martyr's death is not the final word. Jesus rose from the dead as the firstborn of many who will follow him in rising from the dead.

The third title for Jesus is the "ruler of kings on earth." This defies the apparent absolute sovereignty of Rome and its leaders—and of any other political leaders. Jesus Christ is ultimately the sovereign one, though in the present only eyes of faith see that.

These three titles are crucial for understanding the whole book. They reflect the pattern of Jesus: faithfulness leading to suffering and even death, leading to resurrection, leading to exaltation and sovereignty. This pattern of Jesus is strongly held up in this book as the pattern also for those who would follow Jesus.

The tenses of the statement in verse 5 ("who *loves* us and *has freed* us") are significant. The love continues and is a present reality even though the act of redemption happened once and for all in the past.

This imagery of liberation is Exodus imagery. This is a theme throughout the book. The act of redemption has already happened in Jesus Christ's work, but the journey through the wilderness in this time before the end is full of dangers.

Verse 6 states that Jesus has made us "a kingdom." This is a political term and refers to the true kingdom as opposed to Caesar's imitation.

Verse 7 tells us that Christ's return will be decisive for *all* people—both those who desire it and those who do not. This is a picture of judgment. A question here and throughout the book is whether this judgment is condemnation or purification—or both. It is not clear if the reference to "every one who pierced him" is for certain people or for all of us, who in some sense are each guilty of killing Jesus.

In 1:8 God is called "the Almighty" or "the ruler of the whole world." This is God's main title in Revelation (4:8; 11:17; 15:3; 16:7; 16:14; 19:6; 19:15; 21:22). It emphasizes that the key issue in the book is *power*—who finally is in control, who has the ultimate power. Is it God or is it Satan and his cohorts?

1:9-11—Occasion for Writing

Verse 9 is important for telling us about John. Like the Hebrew prophets (and unlike the authors of the apocalyptic books), John identifies his own standpoint in his own day. His "words of prophecy" seek to strengthen the congregations in Asia Minor in their severe clash with the anti-God and dehumanizing powers of their society. He gets his authority not only from his prophetic inspiration, but also from his solidarity with the Christians to whom he is writing.

Therefore, he does not introduce himself as prophet or teacher or elder, but as their brother and partner.

He shares in their suffering, as he is exiled on the island of Patmos, which was in the Mediterranean Sea not too far from the city of Ephesus. Patmos conceivably was a place where political prisoners were sent. So John possibly was sent there as punishment for his testimony to Jesus.

John characterizes the Christian life, in 1:9, as "the tribulation and the kingdom and the patient endurance" shared in Jesus. As John sees it, the suffering Jesus' followers face as a result of their faith is not merely a qualifying test through which they are required to pass before they can achieve their promised rule with Christ. He sees tribulation and kingdom as two sides of the same coin. Those who endure with Christ also rule with Christ in the very midst of their suffering.

Verse 10 tells us that John was not just a passive recipient of this revelation. He was actively seeking the Lord when the revelation came.

1:12-16—Initial Vision

These verses contain the first vision in the book, a vision of the exalted Christ. The images in the vision are drawn mainly from Old Testament prophets like Ezekiel, Daniel, and Zechariah. But all are reshaped by John. This indicates that he was not drawing directly on them but rather that they were part of his consciousness and resurfaced during his vision.

The images are impressionistic, not precise. They show things like Jesus' closeness to the churches (walking in the midst of the candlesticks, 1:13), dignity (wearing a long robe, 1:13), purity (white head and hair, 1:14), power (voice like the sound of many waters, 1:15), and his identification with the discerning word (the two-edged sword coming out of his mouth, 1:16).

The seven golden lampstands (1:12) are seen as the seven churches (1:20), meaning the entire church. The image may come from the golden lampstand with seven lights that stood in the Jewish temple (see Exod. 25:31; Zech. 4:2), implying that the church is the new spiritual temple. Since John was writing after A.D. 70 (when the temple in Jerusalem was destroyed by the Romans), it was especially important to see how the presence of God might be felt in the new situation.

It is significant that the first statement that John makes about the heavenly Christ is that he saw him "among the lamps" (1:13, NEB). The first characteristic of Christ revealed to John in the vision is that Christ is present among the earthly congregations of Christ's people. This must be remembered as we look at the rest of the book and its various pictures of judgment and destruction that occur on earth.

1:17-20—Effect of Initial Vision on John

The overall effect of these verses can be one of terrifying majesty; John falls down "as though dead" (1:17). Jesus, the Son of Man, is exalted. But he remains the Jesus of the Gospels: "Do not be afraid," he comforts John.

In 1:18 we again see the threefold conception of Jesus Christ: he is the living one who gave up his life as the faithful witness; he is the one who rose from the dead and is alive for evermore; and he is the exalted one who holds the keys to Death and Hades. The possession of the "keys of Death and Hades" was, in Jewish thought, the sole prerogative of God. Thus, Jesus, is identified as God. Possession of the keys is connected with Jesus' victory over death.

In 1:19 John is told to write. This again indicates that he saw himself as God's servant and that he sees this book as God's message and not his own. What John sees is a series of visions that are all equally concerned with interpreting the past, present, and future.

Summary

This chapter establishes that the book is a prophecy. Prophets are those who see into the realities that lie behind the appearances of this world and set them out, with the consequences they see, so that people may act accordingly. What matters is the truth of the prophet's vision of God's nature and will, and of the world in that light. The spiritual gift of the prophet has more to do with interpreting the present than with predicting the future.

This chapter emphasizes that the book is supernaturally given, comes in letter form, contains an urgent message, and proclaims the centrality of Jesus Christ.

From the start, the key motifs are the progression of faithfulness leading to suffering, leading to resurrection, leading to exaltation. This is the pattern of Jesus and is expected of his followers. This is meant as an encouragement and a challenge to them. John is the readers' brother and partner. He is their peer in many ways. God and Jesus are glorified, not John.

Meditation

Many Christians see Revelation as a closed book. For instance, John Calvin wrote commentaries on all the books of the New Testament ... except Revelation. Many of the visions and images in the book seem to make no sense at all, and a surface reading gives one a picture of God which is not very attractive. Few people see Revelation as having much, if any, relevance for our day-to-day lives.

But the book itself seems to have a different idea. "Blessed are those who listen to the words of this prophecy and keep what is written in it" (1:3, my paraphrase). It is important that we have the correct idea of prophecy. Much more than predicting the future, the biblical prophet was one who preached the word of God in the present. The prophet's job was to challenge people in the present with the claims of God.

The prophecy contained in the book of Revelation has the primary function of challenging Christians with the message that Jesus is the Lord of history and God is working God's purposes out, even though it may not always be readily apparent how this is being accomplished.

The "blessed" people are those who *keep* what is written here, who order their lives according to the prophet's message. Revelation gives us moral instruction, not just abstract knowledge. The message of Jesus and of the rest of the Bible can only be understood as we obey it. Our challenge is not so much to decipher the various visions and images found in this book, but to live according to the light we do see here— and in the gospel in general.

The central focus of the first chapter of Revelation is on Jesus. In 1:5 we are told three things about Jesus: He is the faithful witness, the firstborn of the dead, and the ruler of the kings on earth.

The Greek word translated here as witness is the same word used for martyr. John, in calling Jesus the faithful witness, is referring to Jesus giving his life for humankind. The word *faithful* is used four times in Revelation and all four times it refers at least implicitly either to Jesus or his followers being faithful unto death. It is this faithfulness that resulted in Jesus being exalted as Lord and it is in following him that his followers worship him.

For the first readers of Revelation, being martyred was a real possibility. But for Jesus himself, the crucifixion was only the final manifestation of a way of life: giving himself to others. Not all Christians are called to ultimate martyrdom. But all are called to what one might call figurative martyrdom. By this I mean growing into a way of life in which we are choosing more and more to give to others, in which we are witnessing to the love of Jesus for all people by our love for all people.

The reason that this kind of life is a possibility for Christians is because of Jesus' resurrection—because he is the "first-born of the dead." True life for Jesus and his followers comes not with the attempted evasion of death, but by going through death and coming out victorious.

The affirmation throughout Revelation of the value of literal and figurative martyrdom only makes sense because Jesus, the faithful martyr *par excellence*, conquered death. It is a central element of Christian faith that nothing in all creation—not even death—can separate us from God's love. The only thing that can separate us from God's love is our rejection of it. To be killed, to lose *our* lives cannot separate us from God. Jesus has conquered death. But hating others, taking other people's lives (either literally in warfare or figuratively by neglect or distain) hardens our hearts and keeps us from being united with God's love.

Jesus shows us the way of love, the way of always seeking the good of his fellow human beings. And his resurrection shows that this is where the true power of the universe lies.

The confession that Jesus is the ruler of kings on earth is another statement of his lordship. I am sure that to John's readers this at times seemed hard to believe given the power of imperial Rome and the decided anti-Christian character of much of Rome's activity. Many readers since then have had similar difficulties.

It seems obvious that this rule of Jesus is in some ways hidden. But because of his sovereignty, we can know that the kings are not ultimate and they are not free from accountability to God. The ironic thing is that the kings on earth, when they rebelled against God and crucified Jesus, sealed their own doom and brought about the ultimate victory of God's love.

One of the main themes in the book of Revelation is the conflict between Jesus' power and rule, and the power and rule of the agents of evil. The latter are variously identified as the dragon, the beast, the false prophet, the harlot, and kings on earth.

The inescapable conclusion of the book is that in this power struggle, Jesus is the victor. The decisive victory has already been won with his death and resurrection. The point, however, is not just that Jesus has defeated evil. It is crucial to see *how* Jesus won this battle. The kind of power wielded by the kings of the earth has, in the end, proved to be powerless. Jesus' apparent powerlessness has proved to be true power.

Jesus did not conquer evil by retaliating in kind. When he was taken and crucified, he did not call down twelve legions of angels to do battle against the great crowd that came to arrest him with swords and clubs (Matthew 26:47-56). Jesus conquered evil by the power of defenseless love which, withstanding all that the powers of sin and death could do to him, Jesus rose alive again.

Jesus' statement that those who live by the sword die by the sword (Matt. 26:52) is a statement about the meaning of history. Civilizations that have depended on the sword have perished by the sword.

The remarkable history of ancient Israel bears this out. Israel survived not because of the king's armies but because of the prophetic word. The armies were defeated and the nation-state of Israel destroyed, but the prophetic witness lived on. So did God's people.

For Western Christians to advocate fighting the evil power of Soviet communism with the equally evil powers of nuclear weaponry and third-world dictatorships is to accept a false definition of power. The sword is actually powerless. It can only destroy. It cannot create.

The book of Revelation is a confession that true power resides in the way of Jesus—in redemptive love, in the following of the faithful martyr. Jesus' statement in 1:18—"I died, and behold I am alive for evermore, and I have the keys of Death and Hades"—is a promise asserting that the way of defenseless love is the way to true life.

Questions for Thought and Discussion

(1) Do you think the early church expected history to end soon?
Were they wrong? Do you now expect history to end soon? What
might end it? Do you think that would be God's will? Why or why
not?

(2) Do you feel "blessed" in reading the words of Revelation
(1:3)? Why or why not?

(3) Can you affirm that Jesus is the "ruler of kings on earth" today? What does that mean to you and how you relate to "kings"?

(4) Do the images of Jesus in 1:12-16 make him more or less
believable to you? What do you think the role of imagination is in
understanding, experiencing, and communicating Christian truth?

(5) What do you make of John's claim that this book's origins
are with God and not human wisdom? How much, in reality, does
this book reflect *John's* mind? How much do you think it reflects
God's mind?

(6) How important is it, in your opinion, to study the Bible "in
the church" as opposed to studying it individually?

(7) What do you make of the "liberation" motif (as in 1:5 and
elsewhere)? What does it mean to you that Jesus has "freed us from
our sins"? Personal only? Church only? Social and political? What
did it likely mean to John? What kinds of "sins" did he have in
mind? (Keep this in mind as the book goes along.)

(8) Why do you suppose John was on Patmos? How could one
preacher in such a small powerless sect have been a threat to the
"powers that be"? Can present-day Christian prophets be threats to
the "powers that be"? If so, how? If not, why not? Who might John's
twentieth-century successors be (e.g., Billy Graham, Jim Wallis,
Francis Schaeffer, Dorothy Day, Jerry Falwell, Martin Luther King,
Jr.)?

(9) Are *we* called to be prophets? If so, what might that look
like?

Revelation Two and Three

Message to the Seven Churches

Study Questions

(1) Find the seven cities mentioned in chapters two and three on a map. Are there other churches in the area? Why do you suppose these seven are selected? Is there any significance to the order in which they are mentioned?

(2) Compare the seven letters. What is commanded and criticized in each church? Do all have both good and bad points?

(3) How is Christ described at the beginning of each letter? Compare with 1:12-20. How does each description relate to the content of the letter?

(4) How is John's pastoral concern reflected in the letters?

(5) What general themes are prominent in these letters? How do they relate to the rest of the New Testament? To the church today?

2:1-3:22—Message to the Seven Churches

The seven letters are addressed to specific churches as communities and to the whole church in general, not to individuals. The reference to "the angels of the seven churches" likely reflects the Jewish idea that angels are spiritual representations of earthly

35

realities. In this context they represent the churches seen as spiritual entities.

The seven cities were all located on a main Roman road and formed a circuit, starting with Ephesus (which was nearest to Patmos). From these centers the whole area could be covered. As such, they were perhaps an already-recognized group. The details of each local situation add up to a unified message for all the churches, which the number seven symbolizes.

The themes in these letters show us what the particular pastoral concerns were for John in writing the whole book. There are four concerns in particular that stand out: (1) For Ephesus it was lack of love. (2) For Smyrna and Philadelphia it was external persecution. (3) For Pergamum and Thyatira it was false teaching and religious syncretism. (4) For Sardis and Laodicea it was spiritual sleep and accommodation to the world. These are the basic concerns that John wants to help his readers with and attempts to do so by communicating the visions of the rest of the book.

The seven letters are constructed in essentially the same way, beginning with a commission, followed by a mention of a characteristic of Jesus drawn from 1:12-18, a commendation for faithful things the church was doing (except Sardis and Laodicea), condemnation for unfaithfulness (except Philadelphia and Smyrna), a correction, a call ("He who has an ear . . ."), and a challenge.

One common term in each letter is "to him who conquers," also translated "to him who overcomes" and "to the victor." This person is the one who is rewarded. The victors are those who keep Jesus' words until the end (2:26), who have shared the victory of Christ (3:21). This, in the context of the book as a whole, is clearly referring to being faithful to Jesus Christ and his will even to the point of martyrdom. The martyrs are those who, clothed in the white robes of victory, have come out of great tribulation and have washed their robes in the blood of the Lamb (7:13-14). They have conquered Satan by the blood of the Lamb (12:11). They have conquered the beast and his image (15:2).

2:1-7—*Message to Ephesus*

This is the letter to the church at Ephesus. Verse 1 pictures Jesus holding stars and walking among the candlesticks (see 1:12,

16). This indicates his presence in the church and that he knows what is going on in the church and desires to be with them. Plus, it indicates his ultimate power over them. Jesus knows their faithfulness. He knows of their strength against persecution and their rejection of false teachers and their ongoing strength. Ephesus was a major metropolis and had two temples devoted to emperor worship. In the midst of this, the church remained vital and pure.

However, they were lacking in love. This lack of love for people was leading to a lack of good works. Apparently hearts in the church were hardened in the battle against persecution and false teaching. Jesus' threat to the church at Ephesus was perhaps the most serious threat to any church: the removal of their candlestick. They would no longer be one of his churches.

Love is not overtly emphasized much in Revelation, but this letter indicates that love is nevertheless assumed to be decisive. Without love, truth and fidelity are worthless.

2:8-11—Message to Smyrna

The title of Christ in the letter to the church at Smyrna is "the first and the last, who died and came to life." This is a word of comfort to a congregation that faced renewed persecution and possible death. The Smyrnans are reminded to follow Jesus' pattern: Faithful life leading to suffering and death, leading to ressurrection, leading to exaltation.

The message to this church is totally positive. Though the church was small and suffering and poor, it was a totally faithful church and was therefore rich in God's eyes.

It is likely that the poverty spoken of in 2:9 was related to the afflictions of the church. They may have experienced confiscation of property, looting by hostile mobs, and difficulty in earning a living in but hostile environment—all because of their faithful witness to Jesus.

One message to the church was that it needed to recognize that while the Roman authorities put them in jail, it was really the devil himself who was behind their plight. The statement that the Smyrnans were to be "tested" (2:10) implies that God would use this to strengthen their faith. One of the purposes of the book as a whole is to show how Satan's hand can be detected in the affairs of the world and how God uses that which Satan does for God's ultimate purposes.

The "second death" referred to in 2:11 is probably the "lake of fire" we read about in chapters 19 and 20. It is a reference to final punishment, final separation from God. The conqueror is immune from this judgment. This was a word of assurance that the first death is not ultimate and that the death that really matters would not touch the faithful ones.

2:12-17—Message to Pergamum

In the letter to Pergamum, Jesus is the one with the "sharp two-edged sword." Jesus is the one who discerns truth and exposes and deals with falsehood. Christ is more powerful than the sword-wielding Caesar. It is Jesus' sword, not Caesar's, that unfaithful Christians should fear (2:16).

The reference in 2:13 to "Satan's throne" could be an allusion to the fact that Pergamum was the Roman empire's regional governmental headquarters. This is where the earliest temple for state-sponsored emperor worship in the area was built. Already one important church leader, the faithful witness Antipas, had been killed—presumably due to his resistance to emperor worship. Still, the church remained true.

However, the church had tolerated false teaching. "Balaam," "the Nicolaitans," and "Jezebel" (2:14-22) all probably refer metaphorically to the same problem: going along with the culture religion in order to participate more fully in the commercial, political, and social life of their cities. One of the specific manifestations was eating meat sacrificed to idols (perhaps at trade-guild meetings, business associations, and private parties). The term translated "immorality" (2:14) probably has the broader connotations of spiritual infidelity. This might be manifested sexually, but was also manifested in other ways.

What the Thyatiran letter says about "what some call the deep things of Satan" (2:24) indicates that these people were probably influenced by gnosticism, a religious movement of that time that emphasized secret knowledge and spiritual achievement and downplayed the physical. Their spirituality would be unaffected by what they did with their bodies.

In both churches, to adhere to these false teachings—or even to tolerate them—would lead to bad consequences. It would turn the church into simply another pagan temple. The church would lose its distinctiveness and its ability to offer an alternative to idol worship and bondage to false gods.

In 2:17 the victor is promised "manna." This is a calculated contrast to the teaching of the Nicolaitans who eat food sacrificed to idols and are doomed to judgment by the sword of the Lord. The victor will eat the bread of heaven and will be sustained in the kingdom by the power of the Lord. The white stones were used as tickets of admission to public festivals. Here they are perhaps a symbol of admission to the messianic feast.

2:18-29—Message to Thyatira

The title of Christ in the letter to Thyatira reminds the readers that the true Son of God is not the emperor or the guardian deity of the city, but the resurrected Christ. The flaming eyes suggest the penetrating power of Christ's ability to see through Jezebel's seductions.

Like the church of Pergamum, the church at Thyatira was faithful in many ways. It did good works, had love, ministry, and patience, and was growing. But also like the church at Pergamum, it tolerated false teaching.

In the Old Testament, Jezebel was the wife of Ahab who attempted to lead Israel into idolatry by the introduction of the cult of Baal. The problem was one of religious fidelity. By using the term "Jezebel," John was emphasizing that religious fidelity was the issue facing the church at Thyatira—whether or not Jesus alone was Lord.

Verses 26 and 27, with their reference to the iron rod, contain interesting imagery. Martyrdom is for the "conqueror" a personal victory over temptation and death, but it is also the victory that overcomes the world. Psalm 2:9 is quoted here. The psalmist looked forward to the day when God's Messiah would "smash" all resistance to God's kingly rule and assume "authority over the nations."

John sees this ancient hope transformed in light of the cross. Pagan resistance will indeed be smashed, but God will use no other "iron rod" than the death of his own Son and the martyrdom of the saints.

3:1-6—*Message to Sardis*

The church at Sardis is "dead." In 3:1 it is therefore fittingly addressed by Christ, who is "the one who has the seven spirits." Only the life-giving Spirit of God in all its fullness can bring the dead to life. Neither persecution nor false teaching is mentioned here. Sardis is simply spiritually asleep. Therefore, nothing good can be said about her.

Twice in the city's history it had been taken unawares and captured by enemies, though it was well-protected. The reference in 3:3 to the church's lack of vigilance and its need to wake up lest it fall under judgment is a striking parallel. Since Jesus tells the church at Sardis to wake up and warns her that his coming to judge her will be quite unexpected, it seems that the church is not aware of its real spiritual state.

The reference to soiling their clothes in verse 4 indicates that while they outwardly maintained their good works and Christian activities, the Christians at Sardis desired to adapt themselves to the luxuries and pleasures of their environment. The few that remained faithful are promised white clothes.

3:7-13—*Message to Philadelphia*

One special problem for the Christians at Philadelphia appears to have been persecution from Jewish people. So the title of Jesus in 3:7 is significant. Jesus is the "key of David" who now opens the door to God for *Gentile* Christians, too. Jesus' work cannot be reversed. He is the only mediator between people and God.

In this letter, like the one to Smyrna, there are no negative statements about the church. "I know that you have but little power, and yet you have kept my word and have not denied my name" (3:8).

In 3:9, we see that the Jewish hope has been turned upside-down. It was not the Gentile oppressors of Israel who needed to recognize Israel's primacy in God's kingdom; it was the Jewish persecutors of the church who needed to see that the church was the new Israel. Christ, "the true holy one" of Israel, loved her in giving his life for her.

The hour of trial referred to in 3:10 is directed toward the entire world, but Christians will be kept safe through it by the spiritual protection Jesus Christ provides against the forces of evil.

"Those who dwell upon the earth" (3:10) is a common phrase in Revelation. It generally refers to those outside the church: its persecutors, the emperor worshipers. Here the reference is to the tribulations revealed in chapters 6 to 20. Faithful Christians are kept from them. They may be affected by them, but they will be kept safe in an ultimate sense. These tribulations cannot separate them from God's love.

The "pillar in the temple" (3:12) and the "new Jerusalem" are promises made to the conquerors that implicitly counter the claims of the Jewish persecutors. They also promise God's continual presence. Nothing can separate the faithful ones from God. "Hold fast"—do not give up.

3:14-22—Message to Laodicea

In the letter to the church at Laodicea, Jesus is the "faithful and true witness" (3:14). This title stands in stark contrast to the useless and tepid church at Laodicea.

Like the church at Sardis, the church at Laodicea is not commended for anything. The only problem mentioned is the church's uselessness—its total lack of good fruit. Nothing is said about external persecution or false teaching. The church may have been comfortable, but it was misled. "You say, I am rich, I have prospered, and I need nothing; not knowing that you are wretched, pitiable, poor, blind, and naked" (3:17).

Apparently the city's water supply came from mineral springs and arrived to the city lukewarm. The water was useful "hot" or "cold," but when it was "lukewarm" it was nauseating and useless. The reference in 3:15, then, may not be to the *spiritual* temperature of the Laodiceans (with the paradoxical statement that Jesus prefers people to be totally cold spiritually rather than lukewarm). Instead the reference is probably to the barrenness of their works—their lack of faithful witness.

The fact that Jesus rebukes Laodicea in 3:19 shows that he still loves the church. The threat of total rejection if she would not repent is balanced by the promise of total reinstatement if she would.

In the chapters that follow, we will see a great deal of trauma and suffering. In the effort to understand and justify it, we need to continually remember what is said here: "Those whom I love, I reprove and chasten; so be zealous and repent." Though not a single positive statement about the church appears here, Christ's love for it is strongly emphasized.

Verse 20 tells us that Christ is present and aware of the church's faith or lack thereof. The promised (or threatened) coming of Christ is not simply a matter of judgment. It is a matter of God's love. If it takes the form of discipline now, it is for the purpose of saving people from exclusion when the door is finally shut.

To those who respond to this message and to God's discipline, the promise is that they will share in Christ's exaltation (3:21).

Summary

The angels of the churches represent the churches as spiritual entities, reflecting an idea common in ancient Judaism that angels were spiritual counterparts to earthly realities. The seven letters are addressed to seven specific churches as communities and to the whole church in general, not to individuals.

The themes in these letters reveal John's particular pastoral concerns in the book as a whole: (1) lack of love; (2) external persecution; (3) false teaching and mixing Christianity with other religions; and (4) lackadaisicalness, spiritual sleep, accommodation to the world. All that happens in the rest of the book should be understood in this light. Revelation as a whole was meant to bring about obedience in the face of these problems.

Each letter refers to "the one who conquers," also translated as "the one who overcomes" and "the victor." This one will be rewarded. The conquerors are those who keep Jesus' words until the end (2:26), who share the victory of Christ (3:21). These clearly are Christians who are faithful to Jesus and his will to the point of martyrdom, the ultimate victory.

The seven letters anchor the book as a whole in actual history. These are existing churches. The rest of the book was meant to help them be victorious in the midst of their real-life problems.

Meditation

These seven messages have universal applicability. Churches of all times and places struggle with focusing on doctrinal purity over love as did the church at Ephesus. It is always a temptation to believe (like the church at Laodicea) that external wealth is a sign of God's blessing and that costly commitment to the way of Jesus is optional. For Christians experiencing persecution for their witness to Jesus, the Lord's words to the church at Smyrna cut to the heart of the matter: "Be faithful unto death, and I will give you the crown of life."

Though these messages do not say everything about church life, they do raise some pertinent issues.

Jesus strongly commends a number of the churches for their faithfulness to his way in the midst of tribulation. The church at Pergamum did not deny Jesus' faith even when one of its leaders was killed. The church at Ephesus was enduring patiently. But the churches at Smyrna and Philadelphia especially gain Jesus' approval. He knows that they have experienced tribulation and poverty in the world's eyes, but he considers them rich. He knows that they have but little power. Yet the most important thing is their faithfulness; that is where true power lies.

Faithfulness in the midst of tribulation is one of the central themes of the book as a whole. It is one that is perhaps a bit difficult for most of us to relate to. How much tribulation do we encounter due to our faithfulness to Jesus? In the way that these early Christians encountered tribulation—the loss of life or livelihood—we probably do not encounter a lot. We could ask ourselves why not. Are we as comfortable as we are because we are not public enough with our faithfulness?

The key point for us is not faithfulness specifically in the midst of poverty and persecution. Rather, the key issue is faithfulness in the midst of whatever temptations the churches face.

These temptations to leave the way of Jesus vary with each church. For the churches at Philadelphia and Smyrna, the temptations were clear. They were tempted to buckle under the pressure of overt persecution. But they were remaining faithful. They were withstanding the temptations. This model gives hope for all Christians who are persecuted. This is the kind of temptation that many of the sixteenth-century Anabaptists faced. Many, like the Smyrnans, were faithful unto death and no doubt received the promised crown of life from God.

Other kinds of temptations also confront the church—ones which these churches (and many churches since then) have not been so successful in withstanding. Instead of being tempted with poverty and persecution, the church at Laodicea was tempted with wealth and toleration. It was apparently not faithful. Jesus calls it "wretched, pitiable, poor, blind, and naked."

It is fascinating, though sad, to look at the first few hundred years of the Anabaptist movement with regard to these two contrasting kinds of temptation. The 1500s saw the rapid spread of the movement as thousands of Europeans were attracted to this new kind of Christianity that seemed to recapture much of the dynamism of the early church. Yet a few hundred years later there were hardly any Anabaptists left, except in eastern Europe and North America.

As I have implied, this was in part due to the faithfulness unto death of many Anabaptists—the refusal to yield to the same temptations faced by Smyrna and Philadelphia. Many were killed or forced to migrate. But many Mennonites, especially in Holland, yielded to the kind of temptations faced by Laodicea. As they gained prosperity and toleration, their faith became lukewarm.

Perhaps the temptations most relevant to us are those faced by the churches at Thyatira and Pergamum. These churches were in many ways faithful to their Lord. But they accepted the teachings of false prophets. They ate food sacrificed to idols and practiced immorality. These things symbolize accommodation to false religions and worldly ideologies.

These churches were willing to tolerate the claims of other gods and other worldviews, along with their commitment to Christ. But according to the Jesus of these letters, this toleration was wrong. His way is the only way. It is to be followed without compromise.

Today in North America, we are not so much tempted by clearly non-Christian worship activities like sacrificing to idols. However, some worldviews (or sets of values), while not claiming to be religious, still make claims on us that are counter to these of Christ. Many accepted values in our culture are actually religious values and tempt us to leave the way of Jesus.

Our challenge is to withstand these temptations. This is one of the main reasons our congregations exist. Together we gain strength to meet this challenge.

What are some of these tempting values? What are our modern-day Balaams and Jezebels?

In times of economic trouble we tend to grasp after our own security first—to join in the panic-stricken stampede for the lifeboats, before considering others.The need for security is a real one, but the message of Jesus here and elsewhere is that true security is found only in living according to his ways. "It is in giving that we receive," as Francis of Assisi said.

The temptation we face is to think that we must cover all the bases for ourselves. When we are thus preoccupied, we lose sight of others, including Jesus. Of course, the corporate expression of this grasping after our own security is seen in our countries' military policies. Our challenge as congregations is to discern how we together can withstand this temptation and direct our concern outward.

Another manifestation of false values that hinders our worship of God is to despair of change in our own lives and in the world. When we despair, we more or less deny that God is at work in the world. To give in to this temptation is to cut off the possibility of God being manifested in us or through us. To believe that the world can change for the better—that God can and does act—is to open ourselves for involvement as agents of this change.

Another temptation we face is the tendency to think that we have fulfilled our obligations when we give financial support to works of service. It is certainly proper to give this kind of support, but most of all God desires our hearts and lives.

The answer to these temptations is simple: those who have ears, let them hear what the Spirit says to the churches. The Spirit says we must repent of our unfaithfulness and follow the Lamb wherever he goes. "The one who conquers I will grant to sit with me on my throne, as I myself conquered and sat down with my Father on his throne" (3:21).

Questions for Thought and Discussion

(1) Do you think that these are literal, historical churches? If so, why were these letters being placed here to anchor the later visions? (I.e., why were the visions placed in a pastoral context?) Do you see anything *pastoral* in what comes later in Revelation? Does

placing the visions in this context increase their relevance for the church today?

(2) Jesus is portrayed as intimately acquainted with, and concerned for, the specific churches. What implications may this picture of Jesus have had for John? Does this intimacy and concern apply to churches today? If not, why not? If so, what are the implications?

(3) How literal were Jesus' threats to the churches? Do you think they were fulfilled in history? Do they apply to all churches? If so, how will their fulfillment be worked out?

(4) What implications for modern-day churches do the values expressed in these letters have? For instance, the weak, persecuted churches are praised the highest. An "obedient" church is chastened for lack of love (Ephesus). A prosperous, "successful" church is condemned (Laodicea).

(5) Why would Jesus be so concerned about doctrinal purity? What do you suppose was at stake in the controversies with the Nicolaitans, Balaamites, and Jezebelians? Do we have similar controversies today (that is, struggles between radical purists and cultural conformists)? Which side would the Jesus of John's letters take? What do you think might be analogous today to eating meat sacrificed to idols?

(6) Should the church in North America be persecuted more? Should your own local congregation be persecuted more? What might lead to increased persecution? Why are Christians persecuted today? Do you think that there are "legitimate" and "illegitimate" causes of persecution?

(7) Does visualizing Jesus as the "faithful and true witness" (3:14) with "the sharp two-edged sword" comfort you or frighten you? Why?

(8) To what was Jesus referring when he repeatedly spoke of conquering? What does conquering look like today?

Revelation Four and Five
Triumph of the Lamb

Study Questions

(1) Is there any significance to the order of the objects seen in chapters four and five?

(2) What is the chief activity in this section?

(3) To what do the "open door" and the invitation "Come up hither" (4:1) refer? Is the phrase "in the Spirit" (4:2) significant?

(4) What do you make of the description of God in 4:3? What imagery is associated with the throne in this paragraph? Why?

(5) Who are the "elders" and "living creatures" in chapter four and what does the number of each mean?

(6) Who is the Lamb? What is his relevance to the scene here?

(7) What is to be understood by the opening of the scroll (5:2-5)? What is meant by "worthy" (5:2)? Does the remainder of the chapter throw any light on its meaning?

4:1-6a—The Setting in Heaven

"Heaven" here (4:1) is likely the same as the "heavenly places" of the Book of Ephesians—not a place without evil, but the sphere of spiritual reality, where masks are off and both good and evil are seen for what they really are.

The first thing John sees in heaven is a throne (4:2), symbolizing the absolute sovereignty of God. The picture of God on the throne is a favorite of John. He uses it ten more times in the book.

In 4:3 John sees a rainbow. This reference is an important reminder of the covenant of God with humanity, made after the Flood, that the waters will never again be permitted to destroy creation (Gen. 9:8-17). The throne is surrounded with the sign of God's mercy. It warns us not to interpret the visions of destruction that follow as though God forgot his promise to Noah.

The 24 elders (4:4) are representatives of the people of God. The image comes from 1 Chronicles 24 where 24 divisions of priests were each headed by a "chief" or "elder." These had to be present in the temple at the great festivals. The "seven torches of fire" which are the "seven spirits of God" (4:5) picture God's active presence in the world, something usually spoken of as the Holy Spirit. This reference recalls Zechariah where the prophet sees seven lamps and hears that they are "the eyes of the Lord, which range through the whole earth" (4:10).

Elsewhere in Revelation, the "sea of glass" (4:6) is: (1) the reservoir of evil out of which arises the monster (13:1), or (2) the barrier that the redeemed must cross in a new exodus if they are to win access to the promised land (15:2-3). In the new heaven and earth there is no more sea (21:1). The sea, whether on earth or in heaven, belongs essentially to the old order and within that order it stands for everything that opposes God's will. Here it serves as a reminder that God's purpose in what follows in the rest of the book is to get rid of that sea.

4:6b-11—Worship for God's Creation

The four living creatures seen in 4:6 are meant to symbolize the entire animate creation. In their ceaseless worship of God (4:8b) they show that nature (including humankind) worships God just by existing.

This passage counters any dualism between nature and grace. God the Creator and God the Redeemer are one. God's redemptive work has to do with *all* creation, not just human souls.

The praise of the 24 elders in 4:11 differs from that of the living creatures in 4:8 in that it is addressed to God and is based on God's work in creation rather than God's divine attributes, thus refuting the idea that God as spirit would not be involved directly in a material creation.

The vision in chapter 4 merges many Old Testament images of divine truth and presents God the Creator as worthy of universal praise (4:11). All that exists is under God's sovereign sway. That is why the divine throne is the central and primary feature of the vision (4:2).

5:1-5—The Dilemma and Its Resolution

In 5:1 John sees God's "right hand." This indicates that the visions are not meant to be visualized in a literalistic way. Rather they are to be interpreted as meaningful symbols—a visual way to present an idea.

The scroll is to be understood as a legal document relating to the destiny of humankind. The content of the scroll is God's redemptive plan, foreshadowed in the Old Testament, by which God asserts sovereignty over a sinful world and achieves the purpose of creation.

The exultant tone of chapter 5 supports the interpretation that the three series of plagues are three pictorial presentations of one reality: the messianic judgments that precede the kingdom of God. The important feature of the sealed document is not the judgments that accompanied the opening of the seals, but rather the supreme event to which they lead (i.e., the coming of the new Jerusalem).

The breaking of the seven seals and the following events do not constitute the content of the scroll but are preliminary and preparatory to the actual disclosure of the scroll's contents. These contents include both the establishment of the New Jerusalem and the destruction of evil. John longed for both of these things to happen.

The big question in the light of this longing is, "Who is worthy to open the scroll and break its seals?" (5:2). That is, who can bring history to a conclusion? Who can bring about final redemption? This question was especially pressing in the light of the apparent failure of the history of Israel.

No one could be found to do so. Apparently nothing could be done. So John "wept much" (5:4).

One of the elders, however, tells him not to weep (5:5). Someone *has* been found: "The Lion of the tribe of Judah, the Root of David, has conquered."

The Messiah has come. The "Lion of the tribe of Judah" alludes to one of the first messianic prophecies in the Bible, Genesis 49:9-10. We know from Jewish literature of New Testament times that the lion was used to indicate the conquering Messiah (e.g., see 4 Ezra [2 Esdras 11:37; 12:31]), even though the metaphor is not found elsewhere in the New Testament. The reference in Genesis is obviously not to a humble, suffering Messiah but to one who wielded the sceptor as a ruling king. The "Root of David" is an allusion to Isaiah 11:1. The royal family of David, the son of Jesse, was likened to a tree which had fallen, but from whose roots had sprung a new tree to restore the kingly rule of David. The verses that follow give a vivid prophecy of the promised triumphant messianic king.

The Messiah had come. The scroll could be opened. But most Jews had not recognized him. No one would say that a conquering king like the one prophesied had come.

The purpose of the titles in 5:5 is not only to assert the Messiah Jesus' authority to open the scroll, but also to set up the contrast in 5:6 with the master title—"Lamb"—which is used throughout the book for Jesus. Conquest is thus tied to sacrificial suffering and apparent defeat. "Lion" and "Root" over against "Lamb" are a symbolic equivalent to Paul's claim that "we preach Christ crucified . . . the power and wisdom of God" (1 Cor. 1:23-24).

5:6-10—*Revelation of the Slain, Triumphant Lamb*

What John hears—the traditional Old Testament expectation of military deliverance—is reinterpreted in 5:6 by what he sees—the historical fact of a sacrificial death. He sees a "Lamb" who bears the marks of slaughter, which are explained by the heavenly choir in 5:9-10: With his lifeblood he has ransomed "for God people from every tribe." The "Lamb" is the symbol of self-sacrificing and redemptive love.

The slain lamb (which John "saw") is interpreted by the Lion of Judah (of which he "heard"). Its death is not weakness and defeat (as it seemed to be), but power and victory. The Lion of Judah, the traditional messianic expectation, is reinterpreted by the slain lamb. God's power and victory lay in self-sacrifice (in contrast with Satan's, whose beast looks like a lamb but speaks like a dragon, 13:11).

The lamb which appears to be slain *is standing.* The slain lamb is the risen lamb. Even apart from the cut throat, this is no ordinary lamb. It has "seven horns and ... seven eyes" (5:6). In the Old Testament horns symbolized power (e.g., Deut. 33:17) and at times royalty (e.g., Dan. 7:7). "Seven horns," then, signifies fullness of strength. The Lamb of God is immensely powerful. The "seven eyes" signify fullness of knowledge (cf. Zech. 4:10).

John is, in effect, redefining omnipotence here. The omnipotence of the Lamb (and hence of God) is not to be understood as the power of unlimited coercion, but as the power of infinite love—the invincible power of self-negating, self-sacrificing love. The gospel sees no other way of victory for the Messiah in overthrowing God's enemies than the cross. This is crucial for understanding the rest of Revelation.

Hints of this can be found in the Old Testament. The lamb metaphor was central in the great prophecy of the suffering servant in Isaiah 53. Isaiah saw one who was humble and despised, who would be abused and maltreated, but who would redeem his people by suffering—bearing their transgressions and their iniquities in his own person. His sufferings would lead him to the point of death. The Jews did not know what to do with this prophecy of the servant of God who suffered the fate of a slaughtered lamb. It could not be a prophecy of Messiah. By definition Messiah was to be a victorious, conquering king who would overthrow the powers of evil (not be crushed by them). There is no clear evidence that the suffering, lamb-like servant was ever applied to Messiah in pre-Christian times by Judaism. The role of the conquering, reigning king and that of the meek, rejected, suffering servant seemed to be mutually exclusive.

But when Christians found Jesus fulfilling Isaiah's prophecy, they began to regard it as a messianic prophecy. This is a dramatic change of imagery in relation to God's work of salvation in the world—one which Christians all too often neglect. God's work is a work of love. The word *love* seems a mockery when applied to the terrible Lamb of chapters 6—20, but his eternal purpose is the redemption of all people, and his severity to those who side with the dragon and his cohorts is a function of that purpose.

In 5:9-10 a new song is raised in thanksgiving for the accomplishment of the promised redemption and the coming of the new age. This song is repeated in 14:3 and 15:3-4 and anticipates the new heaven and new earth, in which all things are made new by God (21:1ff.).

Jesus is praised in 5:10 for what he *has* achieved. The ransomed are *already* "a kingdom," sharing Christ's pattern of kingship (1:9) in faithful "witness to the truth" (cf. John 18:37). As "priests" they are to bring the obedient worship of the nations to God—again through their witness. Their kingship and priesthood are yet to be fulfilled, but it is crucial for our understanding of John to recognize that he could regard it as in some sense being a present fact.

5:11-14—*Worship for God's Redemption*

The Lamb is worthy to take the scroll, break the seals, and eventually open the scroll, thus bringing history to its consummation (5:12). This symbolizes Jesus' redemptive work and eventual destruction of evil. Because of what he has done, *all* creation worships him.

Verse 13 presents a positive picture. *Every* creature worships God and Jesus. The Lamb's work is good news for every creature, person or animal. Whether everyone will actually recognize this is another matter. But the threats and images of destruction are threats of what might be, not promises of what will be. God's will is always that everyone repent and join in this worship (9:20, 21; 16:9, 11).

Summary

These chapters contain visions developing the statement of Christ in 3:21 that he has conquered and therefore shares in the throne and power of God. This is a very important section of the book. It provides the key to understanding the plagues that follow in chapters 6 to 20:

(1) God is the Creator and Redeemer and is in ultimate control of history. The plagues are not outside that control and ultimately serve God's creative and redemptive purposes.

(2) Christ the Lamb acted decisively prior to the plagues to win the crucial victory over Satan with his death and resurrection.

(3) In doing so, the Lamb set in motion the series of events that

will culminate in the destruction of evil and the establishment of the New Jerusalem on earth.

The end result of all this activity is that "every creature in heaven and on earth and under the earth and in the sea, and all therein," sing praise to God and the Lamb. In spite of the plagues, all creation ultimately worships God for God's work through the plagues.

Meditation

Our culture is characterized as lacking hope for the future. No longer do people believe in the American dream of prosperity and happiness for everyone. Our economy is disintegrating. Bridges, roads, sewer systems, and train beds are all falling apart. The environment is being damaged.

Overshadowing all of this is the threat of nuclear holocaust. In a recent poll, 83 percent of a representative sample of Californians indicated expectation of nuclear war in their lifetimes and do not expect to survive it. This expectation cannot but affect how people think about the future. What results for many people is nihilism: nothing really matters and we cannot do anything about it anyhow, so who cares?

Human beings, however, are not created to be hopeless. Where there is no hope, there is no life. To be without hope is to be dead, to be miserable motion machines.

Revelation 4 and 5 help us in understanding how we can receive the gift of hope. Chapter four reemphasizes in symbolic imagery the common biblical theme that God is the Creator and that creation by its very existence worships the Creator. This idea of God as Creator is very important in understanding how and why we can have hope in our lives. To say that God is the Creator is already to say that life and history have meaning and purpose. The universe and human life did not just randomly happen without purpose, but with a random end.

To say that our universe and life itself are created by God is to say that life has meaning and is good. God created life for a purpose. This creation has a beginning and is moving toward a goal. Human history is not just a mist, coming with the dew during the night and fading away with the morning sunshine. Rather, human history began with a loving and creative God who is guiding that history toward a goal and who created each of us to play a part in that history.

However, that God is Creator (and that life has meaning in line with the purposes of this Creator) is not always obvious. That life often seems meaningless and hopeless is an indication that something is wrong—that the original goodness of creation has in some way been marred.

Somehow evil has invaded the universe. We are not told in the Bible exactly how this could have happened, since God is good and creation is good. Evil remains a mystery. The story of Adam and Eve shows us, though, that evil is related to human freedom. God created us with an ability to choose, to grow, and to have free, loving relationships with God and with one another. But this freedom has its risks, for we can reject God's love and thus become separated from God.

The whole story of the Bible, however, shows God continuing to woo humankind, seeking reconciliation and restoration. God's intentions are revealed in the covenant with Noah in Genesis 9 after the Flood. God promised to never again destroy the earth: "This is the sign of the covenant which I make between me and you and every living creature that is with you, for all future generations: I set my [rainbow] in the cloud, and it shall be a sign of the covenant between me and the earth" (Gen. 9:12-13). The Creator and Judge is ultimately the Reconciler and Redeemer.

"Round the throne was a rainbow"(4:3). This significant reference reminds us that God remembers the covenant made with Noah, that God will not destroy the earth, that God's will is redemption and reconciliation.

This sign of the rainbow is an interpretive key to the visions of destruction that are given in chapters 6 to 20. In those chapters is a battle between the spiritual forces of good and evil. Evil is ultimately destroyed. Certainly this battle affects the material world. For one thing, real people, like you and me, who are living faithfully to the way of the Lamb, are being warred upon in these chapters by the agents of evil (the dragon and the beast). However, in the end the material world is not destroyed; it is preserved and renewed as the New Jerusalem comes down to earth (21:2).

The New Jerusalem is not yet fully realized, however. There is a longing for it, as there has been for thousands of years. In 5:1 we read that the one on the throne has in his right hand a scroll. This scroll appears to be some sort of legal document relating to the destiny of humankind. Perhaps what it contains is the message of the final reconciliation of all things to God—a final redemption. If so, the opening of this scroll would be the fulfillment of the hopes of all those who trust in the final victory of God's love.

Verse 3 tells us, however, that "no one in heaven or on earth or under the earth was able to open the scroll or to look into it, and [John] wept much that no one was found worthy to open the scroll or to look into it." The scroll remained closed. The story of redemption remained untold. The longing for wholeness remained unfulfilled as long as no one could be found to open the scroll.

Why could not the one on the throne open the scroll. The answer is tied in with the meaning of the creation of humankind as free creatures. Evil came into the world as the result of the exercise of that freedom. It can only be overcome by freely choosing God over evil. But no one was found, it appears, who could do that in an ultimate sense.

"Then one of the elders said to me, 'Weep not; lo, the Lion of the tribe of Judah, the Root of David, has conquered, so that he can open the scroll and its seven seals' " (5:5). Deliverance is granted and salvation is come. Evil has been defeated and the story of redemption is told.

These two descriptive phrases—"the Lion of the tribe of Judah" and "the Root of David"—are two basic images in the Old Testament for the messianic hope held by the people of Israel. The victor here in Revelation 5:5 is a conquering king who wins a military-like victory, thus gaining the power to open the scroll through brute strength.

Verse 6, though, turns the picture upside down. John *hears* "Lion of Judah, conquering king," but what he actually *sees* is shockingly different. "Between the throne and the four living creatures and among the elders, I saw a Lamb standing, as though it had been slain" (5:6).

This is one of the most important visions in the whole book. The power of God to fulfill the hopes of humankind is seen most centrally in the slain lamb. Ultimately, God's power is not the kind of power that forces people to go along through brute force. Rather, it is the power of unshakable love. God wins people over by loving them and inviting them to choose the life that is found in God.

All the forces of evil could not conquer this love by killing Jesus, the Lamb. He conquered evil not by retaliating in kind, but by remaining faithful to the way of noncoercive love, overcoming death in the resurrection.

The Lamb is worthy to take the scroll. The Lamb has true power, because it was slain. It is important for us to realize that this was not an isolated act, something the Lamb did so that none of his followers would have to. In chapters two and three, Jesus called upon the seven churches to be overcomers, even to the point of their being slain, of being martyrs. They were to follow the footsteps of Jesus, the faithful martyr witness.

That kind of overcoming power is available only to those who have true hope. True hope comes from a faith encounter with God—an encounter which helps us to know God as Creator, as the one who made us for a purpose: to reign on earth. This reign, this kingdom of which the living creatures and elders sing, is founded on care and love, not on coercion and force.

The gift of hope comes when we order our lives according to the values of God's kingdom. When we are living lives of love and compassion—forgiving as we have been forgiven, being merciful as God is merciful—our eyes will be opened to see that the Lamb that was slain *is* victorious, that no earthly power can separate us from God's love. As we follow the way of Jesus and grow into unity with him, we see in the rainbow that God, not the nuclear bomb, is Lord of history—and we will be empowered to live our lives knowing that our hope is not in vain.

Questions for Thought and Discussion

(1) Do you believe that the rainbow covenant (cf. Gen. 9:8ff.; Rev. 4:3) is still in effect in this nuclear age? Does the nuclear threat throw it into question?

(2) Can you relate to the worship of God in 4:8-11? Do you visualize God as a being on a mighty throne? What value, if any, do you see in this imagery?

(3) If the interpretation that creation worships God is true, what implications might this have for our concern for the environment?

(4) Does it make sense to you that a slain lamb could determine the outcome of history? How would you explain this affirmation to a non-Christian? Does this have any implications for the style of our discipleship?

(5) Do you agree that the "Lamb" here is the symbol of self-sacrificing and redemptive love? Why or why not?

(6) Do you agree that the true understanding of divine omnipotence here is that of infinite love and not unlimited coercion? Does that go counter to your assumptions regarding God's almighty power? What are the implications of this view for how we think of God's role in our world and in our lives?

(7) Does the idea that Jesus has made people a kingdom (5:10) seem far-fetched to you in the light of your awareness and experience of brokenness, imperfection, and evil in the world? What might this claim mean?

Revelation Six and Seven

The Seals

Study Questions

(1) Note the language of "seeing" and "hearing" used in this section. How is this to be understood? Can the geographical setting be reconstructed? Where is the speaker? The hearer? Where do things happen?

(2) Are the various roles of the Lamb in chapters 5, 6, and 7 contradictory?

(3) What significance, if any, should be attached to the color of the horses? What is associated with each horse? What calamities accompany the four horsemen? Compare with Mark 11:8. Compare 6:2 with 19:11. Do you see any relationship?

(4) Why the reference to the altar in 6:9? Why are the martyred souls under the altar? Is their cry a Christian one (6:10)? Why or why not? What general conditions does the chapter describe (see 6:9-11)?

(5) What sort of imagery is employed with the opening of the sixth seal (6:12-13) and what is its meaning?

(6) What are the two foci of interest in chapter 7?

(7) What significance, if any, is there in the four horsemen in chapter 6 and the four angels in chapter 7?

(8) What is meant by the "sealing" in 7:3-8? Who are sealed?

Why? Is the number and distribution of the sealing significant? What appears to be its purpose?

(9) What relationship, if any, is there between the sealed (7:4) and great multitude (7:9)?

(10) What is said about the status, activity, and experience of the great multitude in 7:9-17?

6:1-2—First Seal: The White Horse

In 6:1, the Lamb opens the seals and suffering and destruction results. On the surface, it would appear that the Lamb causes the destruction—that this is how the Lamb actively judges a sinful world and that the image of "Lamb" is transformed into the image of a violent, conquering, wrathful judge.

This is a vision of human reality as it almost always has been. Wars, famine, rebellion, disease, and tremendous social upheaval are characteristic of all eras of the past and are certainly characteristic of our day. So what is pictured here is not something unusual. John was simply seeing reality—pictures of what has happened and will continue to happen. These things are evil. But John also saw the Lamb opening the seals, affirming that God uses these evil things to bring about God's purposes. The prime example of this is the death of Jesus. Evil caused it, but God brought good from it.

[handwritten margin note: God doesn't make the things happen — but he makes good outcomes]

Jesus did not merely defeat the powers of evil; he made them agents of his own victory. This is why John says that Jesus "has won the right to open the scroll," and why the scroll, once open, lets loose upon the earth a series of plagues. John is not asking us to believe that war, rebellion, famine, and disease are the deliberate creation of Christ, or that—except in an indirect way—they are what God wills for the people he has made. They are the result of human sin. The point is that just where sin and its effects are most in evidence, the kingship of the crucified is found, using human wickedness in the service of God's purpose. As we proceed, we will see evil serves God purposes (e.g., killing of Jesus and the testing of Christians). The folly of worshiping false gods is exposed. Evil punishes and eventually destroys itself.

The interpretation of the first horseman (6:2) is controversial. Some say that because the horse is white it must indicate the "conquering" gospel, which Mark 13:10 tells us will spread in the last days along with the spread of evil.

Others see the first horseman as evil, representing wars of conquest. The basis for this interpretation is the need for consistency with the other seals and and with the other series of seven plagues that come later in the book, the trumpets and the bowls. The white horse could be part of the imitation motif of the dragon, which we will look at in later chapters. I accept this latter interpretation.

When taken together, the four horsemen represent war and its attendant evils: war, strife, famine, and disease. The white horse signifies triumphant warfare. The horseman rides victoriously on his career of conquest.

"Conquer" is used 11 times in the book to allude to conquest by a faithful witness (once in each of the seven letters, in 5:5 of the Lamb, and in 12:11 and 15:2 of the faithful servants). Three times it refers to conquest by violence (here, in 11:7 where the beast kills the two witnesses, and in 13:7 where the beast wars against and conquers the saints). In all "conquering" passages, Christ and his followers conquer by dying; Satan and the evil powers by killing.

6:3-4—Second Seal: The Red Horse

The language in these verses suggests that the first rider represents an army invading other countries from the outside (the rider is "bent on conquest"). The second represents a general confusion of strife including perhaps civil war or revolution ("that people should slay one another"). The two signs follow the pattern of Jesus' apocalyptic discourse in Mark 13, Matthew 24, and Luke 21, where we read of "wars and rumors of wars" (i.e., wars near and far): "nation will rise against nation, and kingdom against kingdom." The second seal extends and intensifies the strife so that all peace is taken from the earth. The red horse probably signifies bloodshed.

6:5-6—Third Seal: The Black Horse

The third rider's horse is appropriately "black," for he introduces famine. The "balance" implies that food will have to be weighed out and rationed with care (cf., Lev. 26:26; Ez. 4:16). The price of wheat and barley indicates that they are scarce. The command, "Do not harm oil and wine," could illustrate that some will self-indulge, even in time of famine.

6:7-8—*Fourth Seal: The Pale Horse*

The last rider, Death, with his accomplice Hades stalking be-hind him—gathers the results of the work of the previous three. John's readers knew that war was commonly followed by pestilence, famine, and wild beasts that multiplied without check. They were also aware of Ezekiel 21:14: "Prophesy therefore, son of man; clap your hands and let the sword come down twice, yea thrice, the sword for those to be slain; it is the sword for the great slaughter, which en-compasses them."

The first four seals do not portray a sequence of events, but dif-ferent aspects of Roman power and rule: the expansionistic military success of the Roman Empire, the inner strife and war which was un-dermining the world-wide Pax Romana, the concomitant inflation that deprived especially the poor of their essential food sustenance, local rebellions, and finally pestilence, death, and widespread hunger. This was the bitter fruit of Rome's wars of conquest. Cer-tainly this cannot be limited only to Rome. It has happened many times since then.

The fact that Death and Hades are the agents here shows that these plagues are evil. They are not obedient angels of God even though they are ultimately used by God.

6:9-11—*Fifth Seal: The Martyrs*

"Under the altar" (6:9) was where the blood of sacrifices was poured out in the Old Testament (Lev. 4:7). Here the faithful wit-nesses are pictured as a sacrifice to God. Their suffering is not in vain. The death of each martyr brings the end closer and thus helps to bring about a new age. This vision expresses the conviction that suffering is not random or meaningless. There is a cosmic plan, a divine providence. Those who keep God's word and witness to the truth need not fear death. They can rejoice in the knowledge that their suffering contributes to the manifestation of God's rule.

Verse 10 is a bit troubling with its call for vengeance. There are at least five possible ways to interpret it: (1) as a call for personal vengeance which God answers in the way that it was intended; (2) as an understandable call for personal vengeance that God answers in God's way; (3) as a misled call for personal vengeance that God answers in God's way; (4) as a call for vengeance against Satan; or (5) as a general call for God's righteousness to win out. Regardless of one's interpretation, 8:3-5 indicates that God does answer.

The answer to the prayer ultimately comes not in the punishment of individual enemies, but in the "judgment of the great harlot" who deceives the nations (17:1—19:2) and the coming of a new order—one of which even the kings of those who dwell on the earth can be a part (21:24).

6:12-17—*The Sixth Seal: Cosmic Signs*

The opening here of the sixth seal seems at first glance to reveal a tremendous physical catastrophe. However, the fact that after "every mountain and island was removed from its place" (6:14), the mountains still remain (6:16), indicates that something else may be in mind. Since the "top dogs" of society are specifically mentioned (6:15), a sociopolitical catastrophe may be intended. Certain things happen in human history as a result of human sin, such as the collapse of governments, social upheavals, and revolutions.

The kings of the earth and the others are pictured in 7:15-17 as being terrified by the face of him "who sits upon the throne." This is another statement about God's sovereignty and ultimate power over the kings and leaders of the earth.

7:1-8—*The 144,000 Sealed*

When the breaking of the sixth seal was followed by signs of the end in 6:17, people cried out in terror, "the great day of their wrath has come, and who can stand before it?" The answer to this question is now given. Those whom God sealed can stand before it. They will be safely preserved from the outpouring of divine wrath, even though they suffer martyrdom.

In chapter six we saw four horsemen, with a veiled reference to divine permission allowing them to ride forth. Now we perceive four winds that have power to harm the earth (7:1), but are controlled by four angels of God. This would appear to be simply a new angle of view. God's control over the horsemen/winds insures that God's church is sealed and secure *before* they go forth to destroy.

Zechariah 6:1-8 records a vision of judgment that connects four horses (white, red, black, dappled) with the four winds of heaven. Interestingly, John here speaks of the four winds of the *earth*.

Perhaps the winds in Revelation, although they are released by divine permission and used as agents of a divine purpose, are in their essential nature earthly—as earthly as those that dwell on the earth and the kings of the earth whom they afflict, for they are evils that have their origin in human sin.

Several texts in the seven letters suggest that the name of God or of Christ may be on the seal (see especially 3:12). If so, this sealing may be a reference to identifying oneself with God in baptism. Our understanding of its significance in this context affects and is affected by our understanding of who the 144,000 are.

John lists the twelve tribes, representing the people of God in the Old Testament. The twelve is multiplied by twelve either to express perfection or in reference to the twelve apostles. Either way, the intended reference is to the whole people of God in the Old Testament and the New Testament. The multiplication by 1000 implies infinity or innumerability.

According to this interpretation, the sealing or baptism refers to all Christians. This new Israel is protected from separation from God in the midst of tribulations (cf. Rom. 8).

The tribes of Dan and Ephraim are not mentioned here. Joseph and Manasseh are listed instead. Both Dan and Ephraim were known for their idolatry. The 144,000 are those who have rejected idolatry (i.e. antichrist).

7:9-12—Innumerable Crowd Worships God

The innumerable crowd of 7:9 and the 144,000 are one and the same. What John *heard* was God's declaration of their total, given symbolically 144,000. What he *saw* was that this definite total is from the human point of view a numberless multitude. Similarly, from God's standpoint they are all "Israel"—God's people. From our standpoint they come from every nation.

John's eye is presented with a multitude he cannot count, as was Abraham's when called upon to look at the stars which signified his descendents (Gen. 15:5). The vision of the white-robed host, purified by martyrdom, reflects Daniel 11:35. The theme is continued in Daniel 12:1-3, where the same persons as registered "in the book" and "like the stars." This is a way of saying, "numbered by God, but uncountable to people."

The multitude holding palm branches (7:9) is an allusion to the Feast of Tabernacles, which was celebrated after the harvest and was an occasion of great rejoicing (cf. Lev. 23:33-36; Neh. 8:13-18). Palm branches were carried and used in the booths raised on the flat housetops. In Zechariah 14:16-19, the Feast of Tabernacles is set in the messianic era.

7:13-17—Survivors in Their White Robes

The vision here refers not only to the glory of eternity, but also to the life of Christians in the world here and now. The point of this scene is that God's people are safe amid the troubles of this world. God spreads his tent over them.

The faithful ones have "washed" and "made white" their robes. Theirs is an active, not merely a passive role. By their faithfulness they join their sacrifice to that of the Lamb. The victors gain their victories by passing through great tribulation, not by detouring around it. They are able to do this only because of what the Lamb has done for them in giving himself to be slain. Verse 14 refers to surviving the tribulation, not escaping it.

In all that follows in the book, John's readers are never to forget that the victory is a spiritual one. It is a victory over all that can seduce and contaminate. The threat of physical death is not what makes the great tribulation so serious. Rather, the most dangerous thing about it is the serious conflict of loyalties. In this conflict, Christians may be in genuine doubt as to where their duties lie, unless they keep clear on the central affirmation of their faith—that the whole truth of God is to be found in Jesus Christ.

Summary

The visions beginning in chapter six are not chronological. When John says "after this . . ." he means what he *saw* next, rather than what *happened* next in time. For example, chapter 6 speaks of destruction, but 7:1-3 says the destruction is being delayed until the servants of God are sealed. The passages 6:12-17; 11:15ff.; and chapter 16 all bring us to the brink of the last day . . . . but then more happens. We will see other examples later in the book. So we have in these chapters different visions of much the same thing. Two simultaneous views of the same reality are juxtaposed—the plagues and the celebration—here in chapters 6 and 7. This pattern is repeated later in the book. Plagues and judgment juxtaposed with celebration and victory in a way reminiscent of the experiences of the churches at Smyrna and Philadelphia. They were weak and persecuted, but rich in God's sight. Even now we can in some sense experience the kingdom.

The plagues are not so much *caused* by God as they are *used* by God. The visions serve as an encouragement to recognize that God is behind our world's wars and rumors of wars in that God somehow uses them to bring about God's purposes, evil as those things in themselves may actually be.

The fifth seal (6:9-11) is an encouragement to John's readers that their suffering is part of those purposes. They are not random or arbitrary, without meaning or value.

The sixth seal (6:12-17) is a reaffirmation of God's sovereignty vis-à-vis Caesar. God's wrath allows evil freedom to destroy itself and to test Christians. It is purifying for the faithful and destructive for evil, exposing it for what it is. In both cases, it is ultimately a work of God's love on behalf of the creation.

Chapter 7 is meant to be a strong word of encouragement and hope. Those who are identified with God and the Lamb are kept safe from separation from God. Though they may suffer, God's love will meet God's people *in* their suffering and help them to go through it.

It is the responsibility of God's people to wash "their robes and [make] them white in Jesus' blood" (i.e., to be and to remain faithful and pure). This is possible because *God* is faithful and is working in the world to bring about the day when "a great multitude which no one could number, from every nation, from all tribes and peoples and tongues" will worship God and the Lamb together.

Meditation

One of the central themes in the book of Revelation is the interrelationship between the outworking of God's wrath in the world and the effecting of God's salvation. At first glance, it would seem that these two actions are almost in contradiction. This tension is quite apparent in this section.

Chapter 6 tells us what happens when the Lamb opens the first six of the seven seals on the scroll given to him by the one on the throne. This scroll should be seen as a legal document relating to the destiny of humankind. It contains the message of the ultimate reconciliation of creation with God. With the opening of this scroll the hopes of all those who trust in the final victory of God's love would be fulfilled.

In chapter 6 is a series of visions. We see here what John saw when the first six seals keeping this scroll closed were opened. What we see, however, seems quite inconsistent with the idea that the scroll contains the message of salvation. Instead, it contains images of tremendous destruction and killing.

How can these images be related to God's work of redemption? Because they picture human history. Wars, famines, disease, and great social upheaval are characteristic of our day. So what is described is not unusual. John is simply seeing pictures of reality.

This is not just a some fantastic vision in an ancient book. Rather, it is of the world we live in, and it addresses our faith in God now. If God is effecting human salvation and moving history toward a redemptive end, how is it that all these terrible things keep happening? What is the relation between the terrible evils and sufferings pictured here and God's kingdom of peace and healing?

The answer to this question is linked closely with the concept of the wrath of God and of the Lamb spoken of in 6:17. In effect, what is said here is that all these terrible things which are so common in our world are the results of the outworking of the wrath of God and the Lamb. In some way, God's work of salvation includes this series of images of destruction that John sees, images which could well be pictures from the evening news or a newsmagazine.

What does it mean that these things are the outworking of God's wrath? What is God's wrath? For one thing, God's wrath is an expression of God's loving, redemptive will. God is not an internally divided being, part loving and part wrathful. Rather, God is wholly active love. But for those who reject God's love, these acts can seem to be acts of wrath.

Perhaps an analogy can help illustrate this. Parents' attitudes toward their children can be loving and their motivation can be that the children experience the best that life has to offer. Yet sometimes the outworking of this love is viewed by the child as discipline and restrictiveness. It is possible for the child to reject love, to become hardened to it, and to be totally blind to the loving intentions behind the discipline.

God's wrath, though, is more than disciplining those he loves. God disciplines people for their own good. But God's wrath also has a destructive element. God is at work destroying evil. Evil later in Revelation is personified in various characters (the beast, the harlot, the dragon). In chapters 19 and 20 we are told that these characters—along with Death and Hades—are all finally destroyed.

The purpose of this aspect of God's wrath is also redemptive. God's wrath, in hating and destroying evil, serves the purpose of cleansing creation, so that in the new creation people from every nation "shall hunger no more, neither thirst any more; the sun shall not strike them, nor any scorching heat. For the Lamb . . . will guide them to springs of living water; and God will wipe away every tear from their eyes" (7:16-17).

It is important for us to realize what God is doing. God is letting evil destroy itself. God is not directly causing wars and famines. God is providentially using these things, which are caused by the forces of sin and death, to lead to the final destruction of the very same forces which cause them.

The ultimate example of God using the forces of evil to destroy themselves is the crucifixion of Jesus. It was in every way an evil act. But this very act is what ensures Satan's destruction and the completion of redemption.

One part of this whole process is especially troublesome: the forces of evil are not the only ones to suffer. If it is true that the tribulations mentioned in chapter 6 are being used by God to bring about redemption, it is also true that they greatly affect all people, even those who are "on God's side."

One message of chapter 6 is that God uses earthly tribulations to bring about redemption. The affirmation of God's ultimate capability to use even the worst events of human history for God's redemptive purposes is something which can provide hope for people of faith. It is an affirmation of faith that nothing can happen to foil God's purposes. This affirmation is essential for us if we are to remain hopeful in the face of adversity.

When I personally experience evil at the hands of another person, I can believe that God will use that occurrence in ways that are ultimately redemptive. That does not mean that I will not suffer. One clear teaching in the Bible as a whole is that God uses suffering for purposes of self-revelation—to both the sufferer and to world. Even in the context of an incredible manifestation of evil, such as the torture and killing of countless Latin Americans in countries such as El Salvador and Chile, one can remain hopeful that the final word, as with Jesus, who was tortured and killed, is resurrection.

The grounds for this hope are made more explicit in chapter 7. Here, in the first four verses, we are told that the servants of God are "sealed . . . upon their foreheads." John *heard* their number—144,000. This number is symbolic of the whole people of God, Old Testament and New Testament, the twelve tribes times the twelve apostles times 1000 (i.e., uncountable by humans).

The whole people of God is what is meant here. This is made apparent by what John actually *sees*: "Behold, a great multitude which no one could number, from every nation, from all tribes and peoples and tongues, standing before the throne and before the Lamb" (7:9).

Verse 3 of chapter 7 tells us that the outworking of God's wrath was to be held back until the multitudes were sealed. This sealing does not mean that God's people will escape the effects of the tribulations. What it means is that, to use the words of the kings of the earth in 6:17, God's people *will* be able to stand before the wrath of God.

In other words, the actions which destroy evil will not destroy those who are sealed by God. The tribulations we experience will not separate us from God's love. That love does not keep us from suffering, but it meets us in our suffering and assures us of God's reality and, ultimately, of God's victory over suffering and pain and death.

According to these verses, the people of God are secure in God's love and God's ultimate care. The multitudes will indeed come out of the great tribulation and be united with God and experience true peace with God. Coming out of tribulation, in the context of this book, means going through it faithfully, following the way of the Lamb.

This passage challenges us to remain faithful to God through tribulations. The victorious multitudes described in 7:14 are those who "have washed their robes and made them white in the blood of the Lamb." It is the responsibility of God's people to remain pure, to identify with the blood of Jesus as that which exemplifies the ways of God and wins the victory over sin and evil.

This call to remain faithful to God is a call to maintain our faith in the victory of God's love even when hard things come our way. It is also a challenge to share in the tribulations of others, to be faithful witnesses to God's love by loving those who are suffering. This is possible because of the security we have: nothing can separate us from God's love.

This has meaning only because of the promise that God is faithful. The bottom line here is that the Lamb *has* already won the victory over evil, even though the full effects of that are still being worked out. Because of this victory, God provides the resources for us to meet the challenge of faithfulness: the power of the Spirit in our lives, the exhortation of fellow believers, and the testimony of Scripture to the way of Jesus.

Questions for Thought and Discussion

(1) How do you reconcile the Lamb of suffering love in chapter 5 with the Lamb opening the destructive seals in chapter 6?

(2) Do you agree with the interpretation that these plagues are essentially pictures of reality—things that have happened and continue to happen? If so, how can God be using these things for God's purposes and not be their author? What about the role of Death and Hades (6:7-8)?

(3) What is God's relation to modern-day evils, like the world wars, the Jewish holocaust, famines in Ethiopia and Cambodia, and the nuclear bombing of Hiroshima and Nagasaki?

(4) What do you make of the contrast in John's use of "conquer" in the book: the Lamb and his followers "conquer" by suffering, Satan and the evil powers by killing? Does this have implications about how we might go about "conquering" today?

(5) How do you understand 6:10? Should we imitate the sentiment expressed there? Why or why not? If so, to whom would we direct it? Is it conceivable that we as wealthy and imperialistic North Americans might be "those who dwell on the earth"?

(6) Has the number to be killed (6:11) been completed yet? What might this mean? Should we seek martyrdom in order to

hasten the day? How does martyrdom bring the new age closer?

(7) In the light of your observations of the world, is it really possible that "the kings of the earth and the great men and the generals and the rich and the strong" could be terrified of the Lamb (6:12-17)?

(8) Who do you think the 144,000 are? Are you part of them? If so, what does that imply about how you should live? What might being "sealed" (7:3) mean? Could this be a source of comfort?

(9) Do you think we should seek to *avoid* tribulation or seek to go through it? What kinds of tribulation should we avoid? Which should we embrace? What enables people to faithfully go through tribulation? What elements make up John's kind of tribulation— natural "evils" which "happen" to us? or suffering we bring on ourselves by working to overcome evil and sin in the world?

Revelation Eight, Nine, and Ten

The Trumpets

Study Questions

(1) What purpose does the period of silence serve in 8:1? From what sphere of Jewish life is the imagery of 8:1-5 drawn? What sort of prayers are in mind in verses 3-4?

(2) What significance, if any, is there in the shift of imagery from "seals" in the preceding section to trumpets here?

(3) What ideas are associated with each trumpet blowing? Is the imagery employed significant? If so, how? What is achieved by the technique of reptition?

(4) What is meant by the following: The "great star" whose name is "Wormwood" (8:10-11)? The "shaft of the bottomless pit" (9:1)? "The seal of God upon their foreheads" (9:4)?

(5) What does the lack of repentance indicate about the intended purpose of judgment (9:20-21)?

(6) What is meant by the statement "that there should be no more delay" (10:6)?

(7) How is the imagery of the scroll in chapter 10 like and/or unlike that of the scroll in chapter 5? What Old Testament passage is recalled in 10:9-10?

8:1-6—*Seventh Seal: Silence in Heaven and Preparation for Trumpets*

The "trumpets" that follow the half hour of prayer (8:2-3) do not give the content of the scroll. They are warning blasts, summoning the world to repentance (see 9:20-21). "Trumpets" were used in liturgy and in war, for victory and for warning.

The saints do not specify what should happen to persecutors (8:3) as the psalmists did. They pray in accordance with Jesus' teaching (Luke 18:1-8). Verse 15 of chapter 11 suggests that "Thy kingdom come!" was their prayer.

8:7-13—*First Four Trumpets: Plagues of Destruction*

The series of seven trumpets and the series of seven seals share a number of characteristics. Both picture trouble and suffering. In each, the fifth section probes beyond the external troubles to the inner characters of people. In each, the sixth and seventh seem to portray some final disaster and what follows it.

The two series are dissimilar also. Whereas the fifth seal shows *Christians* suffering (6:9), the fifth trumpet shows the world of *unbelievers* suffering (9:4), as do all the trumpets. The last three of them are expressly against "those who dwell on the earth" (8:13; cf. 6:10). The plagues of trumpets one through six recall the plagues that came upon unbelieving Egypt (8:7-9, 12; 9:3; cf. Exod. 7-10). The humans in these trumpet visions are either destroyed by the plagues or unrepentant in spite of them (9:20-21). The coming of the kingdom of Christ, with trumpet seven, is a "woe" (11:14). It could only be such to unbelievers who refuse to repent.

These differences between the two plague series actually support their unity. It would seem that they are two sides of one reality. Suffering is the fate of the world in general (the world in the sense of God's creation, including the church); that is what the seal plagues show. It is also the fate, with a special divine purpose, of the world (in the other sense, of ungoldy human society); that is what the trumpet plagues show.

The sounding of the trumpet (8:7) has several associations, especially with war, in declaring a state of emergency and summoning people to battle (cf. Judg. 3:27ff.; 7:8ff.; Neh. 4:18). It was natural for the prophets to use the symbolism of sounding the trumpet when warning people of the approach of God's judgment (cf. Ezek. 33:1ff; Zeph. 1:15; Joel 2:1). But the trumpet that sounds the alarm for some people, signals the coming of a day of gladness and victory for others (cf. Num. 10:10; Lev. 23:24; Joel 2:12ff.).

The ten plagues against the Egyptians which preceded the Exodus (Exod. 7-10) seem to be adapted in the trumpet plagues. With each trumpet judgment, the devastation is restricted to one third. The plagues are not total; for the goal is repentance.

The hail, fire, and blood (8:7) would seem to symbolize any kind of destruction that at any time damages the earth on which people live (cf. Exod. 9:24ff.).

The effect of the second trumpet (8:8-9) recalls the first of the plagues of Egypt (Exod. 7:20ff.). The particular mention of the loss of shipping may indicate that while the first plague was directed against the human environment, the second was directed against commerce.

The third trumpet (8:10-11) signals the poisoning of the fresh waters. The rivers and springs from which people drink are rendered useless, perhaps symbolizing the destruction of the natural resources that sustain human life. The darkness of the fourth plague recalls Moses' darkening of the sun in Exodus 10:21 and following. The importance of the plagues that struck Egypt was precisely that people could not understand how they happened and had to admit that God was at work (cf. Exod. 8:7, 18-19).

Verse 13 serves as a transition between the four plagues brought upon nature and the following demonic woes in which people will be directly attacked. The previous plagues have been called forth by angelic beings, but those that follow are announced quite appropriately by what seems to be a bird of prey hovering overhead.

9:1-12—*Fifth Trumpet: The Abyss Opened*

The process of retribution is controlled and limited by God. The angel may open the "shaft of the abyss" only because he is "given the key." The "locusts torment" people "for five months" only, and then only because they are "allowed." Just as the natural plagues were limited in scope to one-third, so this plague is limited in time. Evil is in its nature self-destructive. But God mercifully limits its effects in order that people may see in their suffering a trumpet blast of heaven calling them to repentance.

The locusts emerge from the pit (8:3), the place of death. The pit is opened by someone who is a "fallen star," no doubt Satan (Luke 10:18; cf. Isa. 14:12). Satan is "given" divine authority to do this. The locusts' appearance is practically indescribable, but their effect is clear: sheer terror.

The faces of the locusts were as people's faces. When John looked directly into the face of the advancing horde, he did not see the torpid expression of the animal world, but the highly intelligent cunning and cruelty of demonic beings. People and animals are combined in a picture both unnatural and diabolical.

9:13-19—Sixth Trumpet: Four Angels Released

Verse 14 contains a reference to the Euphrates River. The river marked the eastern frontier of the Roman Empire. Beyond it lay the Parthians, the dreaded and mysterious enemy of Rome. Also, the Assyrians and the Babylonians had come from beyond the Euphrates in Old Testament days. An invasion from the east was something greatly feared—both in the past and in the present—for John's readers.

The number four, used of the angels here (9:14), seems to be the number of the earth (four corners, four winds, four living creatures) and perhaps means that these angels represent all the armies of the earth. This idea is supported by the unexplained shift from the four angels to an innumerable number of cavalry (9:16).

The aim of the visions of these plagues is to shock people into avoiding the action—or inaction—that would bring the plagues about. John was not threatening pagans, but revealing to Christians the spiritual nature and destiny of the world to which they were tempted to conform.

9:20-21—Refusal to Repent

The people's refusal to repent implies that they have been offered that opportunity through all of this. Humankind, through its sin, does bring all sorts of evil and horror upon itself. Yet in the grace of God, that trauma could have a positive effect and outcome . . . *if* people would let it work the way God is trying to work it.

However, just as the Egyptians stubbornly resisted God's will, so does John expect humanity to continue in its idolatrous obstinacy. These verses express his conviction that the people of his day were so alienated from the Creator that no crisis would move them to repentance. Events in which the faithful see divine providence and justice are simply blind fate to those without faith. In spite of John's negative expectation expressed here, the door to repentance can always be opened, and Revelation shows us that Jesus continues to knock.

The death-dealing horsemen of trumpet six (9:13-19) represent not only tanks and planes, but also cancers, road accidents, malnutrition, terrorist bombs, and peaceful demises in nursing homes. Yet the rest of humankind, who were not killed by these plagues still does not repent of its idolatry (i.e., centering life on anything but God).

The call for repentance also involves preaching the gospel throughout the world. God's action is not just negative. God offers people a positive alternative to their self-destructive lifestyle.

10:1-7—The Angel with the Little Scroll

Verses one and two show us an angel wrapped in the cloud of God's presence. Over his head is the rainbow of God's mercy (cf. 4:3). The angel bears delegated attributes of deity, but it is also the angel of Jesus Christ, whose face John has seen shining like the sun (cf. 1:16). The legs like pillars of fire are reminiscent of Israel's journeys through the wilderness. This is the angel who is to guide the new Israel through the darkness of its Exodus pilgrimage from Egypt to the Promised Land.

This dramatic appearance of an authoritative figure from heaven stands in marked contrast to the rebellious idolatry immediately preceding (9:20-21). God is still ultimately in charge.

It is not God's patience, but people's ability to respond that is exhausted. There is no point in offering further opportunities, for people have hardened themselves beyond the possibility of repenting. The angel then swears that trumpet seven shall no longer be delayed.

It is most plausible that the seven thunders (10:4), like the seals and trumpets, form another series of warning plagues. The people's adamant decision not to repent (9:20-21) renders another series useless. It is too late to record any further warnings. In the verses that immediately follow, an angel under oath will declare that there shall be no further delay (10:5-7).

"The mystery of God" (10:7) is not truth about God which has not been fully revealed, but is simply the gospel. (Cf. other uses in the New Testament of the word *mystery.*) In verse 7, the word *announced* is actually *euēngelisen*, "preached the gospel."

With the sounding of the seventh trumpet that which God purposed in creation and made possible through the blood of the Lamb (5:9-10) will be brought to its fulfillment. That this purpose is in fact the kingdom of God is clearly seen in 11:15 where following the seventh trumpet the heavenly voices proclaim: "The kingdom of the world has become the kingdom of our Lord and of his Christ, and he shall reign for ever and ever."

10:8-11—*John Commissioned to Eat the Scroll*

The handing of the scroll to John is significant. This represents not just the passing on of a note for communication to the churches; rather, John is being given a prophetic commission, like that which Ezekiel received when he became a prophet (Ezek. 3). As if to underline this, John is told, (like Jeremiah in his call to be a prophet, Jer. 1:10), that he must "prophesy about many peoples and nations and tongues and kings." This clearly has to do not with 11:1-13, but with the later visions of Revelation, notably with those in chapters 13, 17, and 19. The little scroll therefore signifies the reaffirmation of John's prophetic ministry as a whole.

John's great scroll in chapter 5 contained the redemptive purpose of God as it was made effective by Christ. His "little scroll" contains the same purpose, to be made effective through the martyr witness of the church. If the redemptive work of Christ is to become operative in the present, it must be through the witness of his servants, the prophets. Accordingly, John is told that he must prophesy "once again," and this time not in words only. John is to "eat" the scroll—to make it a part of his inmost being. The word of grace must be spoken by the prophet martyrs not only with their lips but also with their lives. This is why the scroll "tasted as sweet as honey" but was bitter to "swallow." The way of victory is the way of the cross.

Summary

The contents of the seventh seal (8:1-6) lead up to the end. The trumpets cover some of the same territory. The trumpets announce the coming of the end. Similar to the opening of the seals, the sounding of the trumpets is not an end in itself.

The first four trumpets proclaim visions of natural disasters which seem to affect all people without distinction. Like the seals, they are the effects of evil and human sin on the world throughout history. The point, like with the seals, is not that God directly causes them, but that they are used by God to bring people to repentance— to test and strengthen Christians' faith, and ultimately to destroy evil.

The fifth and sixth trumpets are specifically aimed at "the inhabitants of the earth" (KJV) (i.e., those who do not know God, those who are the opponents of the faithful).

The picture is one of extreme evil. The imagery is realistic but scary: locusts, scorpions, and invaders from the east (like the Assyrians, Babylonians, and Parthians).

Visions are a graphic attempt to portray the reality of spiritual evil and the promise that God is judging it. The purpose is threefold:

(1) to warn Christians who were being tempted to conform to the evil culture;

(2) to promise that this evil is not ultimately independent of God's purposes;

(3) to indicate, as verses 9:20-21 show, that God invites repentance. (Note the preaching of the gospel that is going on simultaneously; cf. chapter 11.)

That the end is indeed coming is indicated in 10:1-7. The "mystery" of God is the gospel of the kingdom. The promised redemption will indeed come to pass.

John's prophetic call is renewed in 10:8-11. This is a call to recapitulate what he has already prophesied *with special attention paid to the nations and the kings.* This is the central focus of chapters 11 to 20. It is not something new—in addition to what he has seen—as much as it is a restatement of what he has already seen with added depth of meaning.

The little scroll is in continuity with the earlier scroll that the Lamb was opening. It is sweet to those who welcome God's kingdom and bitter to those who reject it. John is to eat the scroll—that is, to fully identify with it and to make it a part of himself.

Meditation

These three chapters picture in various ways the outworking of God's judgment on the world. The trumpet series is the second of three plague series. Many questions arise which are common to all three. One of the most obvious questions has to do with what these visions imply about the relation between God's mercy and God's wrath. Can this God be the same God of love who Jesus and Paul taught about—the God of the suffering love of the cross, who loved his enemies so much that "while we were yet sinners Christ died for us" (Rom. 5:8)?

People who would argue that the God of the plague visions is still ultimately a loving God see an intimation of that in 9:20-21, though the argument is based more on the final outcome of the book. These two verses in chapter 9 interestingly imply that one of the purposes of the plagues is to facilitate human repentance.

However, the people refuse to repent, even after six terrible trumpet plagues. These verses underline the corrupting, blinding, possessing nature of false worship, of people "worshiping demons and idols of gold and silver and bronze and stone and wood, which cannot either see or hear or walk" (9:20). This worship blinds these people from the fact that evil powers are leading them down a path of self-destruction and that the only way out is to turn to the Creator-Redeemer God revealed in Jesus.

John's point here is the same as elsewhere in the book when he pictures the earth dwellers in unfavorable terms. He wants his readers are not to speculate about the fate of those people or to gloat over that fate. Rather, John wants the people *in* the churches to realize what is at stake in their choices. Will they follow the way of the Lamb consistently? or conform to the ways of the surrounding world?

This continues to be his message to us. False worship continues as a tremendous temptation for God's people. What makes this temptation so serious is the subtle nature of various types of worship. This temptation becomes more apparent when we understand worship in terms of ultimate trust. What determines our choices in life?

What really shapes who we are deep down and what we are becoming? If we are honest, I think that all of us have to admit that many things other than God's will revealed in Jesus enter into our decision- and value-making process.

Three idols tempt many of us in modern-day North America. These are not immediately seen in religious terms, but if our "religion" is that which we value most, the connection is readily apparent. These three idols are money, war, and social acceptance.

The first idol is bought to mind by John's reference to "gold and silver." As the first letter to Timothy asserts, "the love of money is the root of all evils" (1 Tim. 6:10). This familiar verse might be a little hyperbolic, but I would argue only slightly so. The problem with money is that it tends to blind us from our basic human vocation: mutual aid, caring for our brothers and sisters. One of the ironies in the story about Lazarus and the rich man in Luke 16 is that the rich man apparently did not even *see* Lazarus begging by his door. When we are burdened by our concern for making and spending money, we are less likely even to be aware of those in need around us.

In our society the vast majority of decisions made by businesses and government are determined by economic rather than "human" considerations. Terms like "the bottom line" and "cost-benefit" analysis are prevalent everywhere, not just in relation to an accountant's work. The priority of money over people is especially apparent in the way large businesses operate. What is especially counter to the values of the gospel is that profit-maximization policies make wealthier a class of people (stockholders) who were already very wealthy as a rule. Meanwhile, the already poor victims who, for example, lose their jobs or have their workplaces and living places polluted for the sake of a few extra percentage points on the profit margin, become poorer.

John's contention here, echoing Psalm 115, is that these idols can neither see or hear or walk. The Psalmist adds: "Those who make them are like them; so are all who trust in them" (Ps. 115:8). When the love of money hardens people's hearts to human suffering and exploitation, when it keeps us from even perceiving the Lazaruses around us, then it is indeed an idol and the root of much—if not all—evil.

John here (9:21) links murder with idolatry. Perhaps one of the clearest indications of humankind's idolatrous commitments is the way that institutionalized murder (i.e. war) is justified and trusted in as an instrument of morality.

Why do individuals prepare for and fight in wars? It is because they give blind trust to their political leaders as the arbiters of (1) who their "enemies" are; (2) and what the appropriate responses to those enemies are. I am convinced of the power of the beast and its false prophet to "deceive those who dwell on earth" is primarily manifested in the war phenomenon.

What are the effects of wars? The death of innocents, destruction of property, reinforcement of reactionary political forces, destruction of democracy, and a general expanding of the power of hatred and violence in the world. Yet people still go on believing in the efficacy—or at least the necessity—of warfare!

The obligation of the God-worshiper is to love God and one's fellow human beings with all of one's heart and all of one's soul. Any human institution which reinforces contrary tendencies is idolatrous. It is from these institutions that the followers of the Lamb are warned to "Come out of her, my people, lest you take part in her sins" (Rev. 18:4).

A third idol is the striving for social acceptance. Behind much of the book as a whole is the concern that God's people were deserting their calling to discipleship in order to become socially acceptable in their culture. This was an especially strong temptation in cities like Laodicea, Sardis, and Pergamum. The cultural conformity was quite subtle, at least in the sense that it was not self-evident to the conformers themselves. "You say, I am rich, I have prospered, and I need nothing; not knowing that you are wretched, pitiable, poor, blind, and naked" (3:17).

People in the church have always had to struggle with the fact that the essential message of Christianity is out of place in this world. The world sees crucified gods, earthen vessels, identification with social outcasts, and such as contrary to the "gospel" of success, power, and prestige. It gives its social rewards to those characterized by the latter set of values, and not the former.

We have to ask ourselves what values are calling the shots in our own decisions regarding how we spend our money, where we live, where we work, what (or even whether) we drive, how we spend our free time, what we say in public, and who our friends and associates are. These things say more than our words about what we worship. Jesus has the strongest words of praise for those Christians who were the least socially acceptable and the strongest words of censor for those who were the most socially acceptable. Is there any reason to think that his words would be any different today?

Questions for Thought and Discussion

(1) What is your emotional response in reading the accounts of the seal and trumpet plagues? Anger? Joy? Fear? Bewilderment? Who do you think causes them and who suffers from them? Do you think they are being experienced in the present? If so, what should our attitude toward them be?

(2) How do you understand 9:4? What do you think of the idea that God causes non-Christians to suffer? Do you want that to happen in history? In eternity? Why or why not?

(3) The trumpet plagues seem to reflect, to some degree at least, the pre-Exodus plagues. In the Exodus account (cf. especially Exodus 7—10), is the key point the punishment of the Egyptians or the liberation of the Israelites? What should our focus be on— punishment or redemption? What role should seeking escape from "plagues" have in the Christian faith?

(4) In 9:13-19 John seems to utilize common social fears to drive home his point about the terribleness of the plagues. What common social fears would a modern-day John play on?

(5) Was John's point to threaten pagans or to warn Christians? Why? What are the implications of your answer for interpreting the book? in terms of applying it to our day?

(6) How do you interpret 9:20-21? God's grace here or only human hard-heartedness? Why does John include this vision? How do you understand the interplay between God's grace seeking people and human rejection of that grace? Could present-day evils lead to repentance? Is it experiencing God's wrath or God's grace and mercy which attracts people to faith?

(7) In the context of these plague visions, 10:1 implies that God still is in charge. How can that be after 2,000 years of continued plagues?

(8) What does it mean (cf. chapter 10) to say that if the redemptive work of Christ is to become operative in the present, it must be through his witnesses, the prophets? How can we "eat" (and thus make an integral part of our lives) the message today? Is it still bittersweet?

Revelation Eleven and Twelve

Spiritual Warfare, Part 1

Study Questions

(1) What is meant by the symbolic action of measuring the temple (11:1-2)?

(2) Who are the two witnesses (11:3) and how is their ministry and subsequent experience to be interpreted?

(3) What is symbolized by the beast (11:7)? Where else is it mentioned in the book?

(4) What is the meaning of the imagery in 11:19?

(5) How is the past tense of 11:15 to be understood in the light of what follows in the remainder of the book? Rethink chapters 4 to 11 in terms of 11:15 as a pivotal point.

(6) Note the imagery of chapter 12. What is its source? How is it developed? Who are the principle actors in the drama? How are they related? Where does the action take place? What results? What clues, if any, are provided for its interpretation?

(7) How should we understand the place references in chapter 12 (i.e., literally or metaphorically)?

(8) What is meant by the war in heaven (12:7ff.)? Is this a reference to a past or a future event? How is the outcome described? Is there any other similar material in the New Testament?

(9) What is the meaning of 12:17?

11:1-3—*The Temple Measured*

In 11:1-2 John conveys the same notion as in the vision of the sealing of the twelve tribes (7:1-8); namely, God will provide for the preservation of the church during the great distress. As the twelve tribes represent the whole church throughout the world, so the temple and its worshipers represent the whole church in all lands.

Between seals six and seven we found those who were sealed serving God in God's temple—in the inner sanctuary. Between trumpets six and seven the unbelievers occupied not only the holy city but even the outer courts of the temple itself. Here too, God's people are safe in the inner sanctuary, which is "measured" (just as its occupants were numbered in 7:4) to indicate that they are all known to God and therefore safe in his care.

In 11:2, the "outer court" and the "holy city," no less than the "temple," symbolize the church in part of its existence. Like the seal which was set on the foreheads of God's servants, the measuring of the temple signifies an inner security against spiritual dangers. But the angel's orders are to "leave the outer court exposed," because God does not offer to the church security from bodily suffering or death. It is God's intention that they should remain outwardly vulnerable to the full hostility of their enemies, secure only in their faith in the crucified and risen Lord.

The court will be trampled for "42 months." This is the same as the "time, two times, and half a time" in Daniel 7:25—that is, three and one-half years, the approximate duration of the persecution of Antiochus IV (the Seleucidian king who tried to destroy the Jews in the 160s BC). It symbolizes, therefore, a time of trial. In Revelation the expression and its equivalent (11:3; 12:6; 12:14; 13:5) symbolically designate the time of trial which separates Christians from the perfect establishment of the kingdom of God.

11:4-14—*The Two Witnesses*

The witnesses in 11:4 are identified with "the two olive trees," which in Zechariah 4 denoted Zerubbabal and Joshua, the high priests, who stood on either side of the lampstand and supplied it with oil. John, however, interprets the olive trees as the "two lampstands." Numerous identities for these witnesses have been offered by commentators over the years. A common futuristically oriented one is that they are two prophets of the last days come to preach repentance in the spirit of Elijah and Moses. Allegorically oriented views have included the Law and the Prophets, the Law and the Gospel, and the Old Testament and the New Testament. But in view of John's earlier use of "lampstands" to represent churches, the witnesses here are most likely the churches of Christ. The number accords with the tradition that valid testimony requires two witnesses (Deut. 19:15).

The witnesses, declaring God's truth to the inhabitants of the earth, are the church in the world—God's people among the heathen nations. They are those to whom the gospel is sweet among those to whom it is bitter, the sanctuary which remains God's own when the outer temple is profaned. They wear sackcloth to show the solemnity of their message.

Inasmuch as the church fulfills the expected ministry of Moses and Elijah, this passage underscores the importance of the church's task as witness. God sends no other agencies to people in the time of the earth's distress than the witnesses of Christ.

Verse 5 recalls Elijah's destruction of the messengers from Ahaziah (2 Kings 1:10ff.) and 11:6 has in view the drought described in 1 Kings 17:1 and the plagues brought about through Moses in Egypt.

The reference in 11:6 to the witnesses "smiting the earth" recalls Isaiah 11:4 where the Spirit-filled descendant of David was to "smite the earth with the rod of his mouth." The church's only weapon is its message inspired by the Holy Spirit, who "convicts the world" (John 16:8ff.) and is a "torment" (Rev. 11:10) to its conscience (cf. Acts 24:25; 1 Cor. 14:24-25). This is not only destructive; for "smiting" may imply "healing" as in Hosea 6:1-5, with reference to apostate Israel (cf. also Rev. 22:2 where the leaves of the tree of life are for the healing of the nations).

In 11:7 the beast symbolizes the power of evil which comes forth to battle God's works. It deceives people and attempts to separate people from Christ's love. The beast is quite active in Revelation from now on and often seems to have the upper hand. But the *Lamb* has conquered.

The city in 11:8 is Rome, but also more than Rome. Like the monster, the great city is a myth which John intends to use to delineate the true nature of Roman imperial power. Rome is simply the latest embodiment of a recurrent feature in human history. The great city is the spiritual home of those John dubs "the inhabitants of the earth." It is the tower of Babel, the city of this world. It has been Babylon, Tyre, and (when it rejected the prophets and then the Messiah) Jerusalem.

The earthquake in 11:13 can be compared with 16:19. The parallelism of these verses and the otherwise consistent symbolism of earthquakes in Revelation are good reason for regarding this earthquake, too, as heralding the end. If the great city of chapter 11 has some of the characteristics of Jerusalem, it also has those of Babylon. John's purpose here is to merge rather than to distinguish the two cities. It is Jerusalem as a rebellious city, not the New Jerusalem, that is in mind.

11:15-19—Seventh Trumpet: The Kingdom of God Established

When the seventh angel sounded his trumpet (11:7), no woe immediately fell upon the people. The woe involved in the seventh trumpet really consists of the seven bowls of 16:1-21.

The central theme of Revelation is the establishment of the kingdom of God on earth (11:15). This involves the wresting of authority from all hostile powers, including the godless nations of the earth, and the exercise of all authority by the "Lord and his Christ."

The end of the age has been reached with the third woe and the seventh trumpet, but it is not described, for we are not yet in a position fully to grasp its relation to history. We shall not be in that position until the contents of chapters 12 to 20 are given. In this passage, as elsewhere in Revelation, the day of wrath is subordinated to the joy of the kingdom of God.

In 11:16-18 the elders thank and glorify God who has at last manifested his great power. The kingdom of God has come. Up to this point, God is described as the one "who is and who was and who is to come" (1:4, 8; 4:8). But here there is no "he who is to come" (cf. 16:5). God *has* come, God's reign *has* begun. Up to this point God has reigned over a rebellious world. A king may be king *de jure*, but he is not king *de facto* until the trumpet which announces his ascension is answered by the acclamation of a loyal and obedient people.

"Destroying the destroyers" (11:18; cf. 19:2) is the key to

understanding the destructiveness of Revelation. John's concern is essentially constructive. God is Creator and Redeemer (chapters 4, 5, and 10). As with the Old Testament prophets, God allows his word in creation to be undone in order that the earth may be purged and re-made (chapters 21 and 22). And it is not as if it were God descending to the level of the destroyers; God allows their work to have its effects, but God's own direct action is different. The "ark of the covenant" (11:19) evokes the redemption from Egypt and the Day of Atonement for which the New Year trumpets prepared, when God wipes out the sins of the repentant.

"Heaven" in 11:19 is not a place of perfection, for it contains war and evil and the forces of Satan. It must therefore be the heaven of earlier in Revelation and of Ephesians 6:12; that is, the sphere of spiritual reality. Consequently, the "temple" refers to the place where God is; not a particular sacred spot officially dedicated to God, but the entire creation. On the spiritual level, there is no place where God is not. The ark is the symbol of God's covenant, or agreement, to rescue his people from their enemies. The lightning, voices, thunders, earthquake, and hail are often used in the Bible as signs that God is present and active—in residence, so to speak, in God's temple.

12:1-6—The Dragon and the Woman

Isaiah 26:16—27:1 forms an impressive parallel to the central thought of Revelation 12. There we have the nation pictured as a woman in labor. There is exultation at the prospect of resurrection, an intimation of the unveiling of God's wrath on the inhabitants of the earth, and a promise that the Lord "will punish Leviathan the fleeing serpent . . . he will slay the dragon that is in the sea."

Regarded as a "sign," the woman is adorned with the splendor of sun, moon, and 12 stars (12:1) which in a parallel Old Testament dream (Joseph's in Genesis 37:9-11) represent the whole family of Israel.

The woman is the mother of the Messiah—not Mary but the messianic community. John makes this clear here by echoing a prophecy about Mother Zion (Isaiah 66:7-9) and later by speaking of the members of the church as "the rest of her offspring" (12:17). She is the Jerusalem above who is our mother (Gal. 4:26). "Her pangs of birth" (12:2) are the suffering endured by the loyal people of God as they waited for their anointed king.

The child is sufficiently identified by the fact that he is to rule all nations (12:5). The original prophecy in Psalm 2:7-9 is declared by many New Testament references to speak of Jesus Christ. It is against him that the dragon's hatred is primarily directed.

By the "birth" of the Messiah John means not Jesus' physical birth, but his cross. In Psalm 2 it is not at his birth, but at his enthronement on Mount Zion that the anointed king is addressed by God, "You are my son, today I have begotten you," and is given authority to smash all the nations with an iron bar.

The dragon's heads (12:3) refer not to intellect but to authority and power. His crowns are royal crowns. His seven-crowned head means that he really does have princely authority (cf., Luke 4:6; John 14:30). The ten horns may indicate that the dragon deploys his authority with very great strength.

In Jewish tradition the serpent or dragon (12:3-4) symbolized the power of evil and the suffering of Israel. Because he is hostile to God and to God's people, God will destroy him at the end of time (cf. Isa. 27:1; Ps. 74:14; Isa. 51:9; Ps. 89:10-11; Job 9:13; 26:12).

The significance of the picture in 12:6 is fundamentally the same as the sealing in 7:1-8 and the measuring of the temple in 11:1-2. During the period of tribulation (the three and one-half years of Daniel 9:27), the Lord's people will experience his protecting care. That this assurance has to be balanced with the implications of verse 11 concerning the church's destiny to suffer is consistent with the juxtaposition of 7:1-8 with 7:13-17 and 11:1-2 with 11:3-13.

In 12:6, the woman (the people of God in the Old Testament which, having given Christ to the world, become the Christian church) found refuge in the desert where God cares for her for 1260 days (three and one-half years), the earthly duration of the church. In the Old Testament the wilderness is the traditional place of refuge for the persecuted (Exod. 2:15; 1 Kings 17:2-3; 19:3-4; 1 Macc. 2:29-30). The wilderness in 12:14 suggests the Sinai wandering. The desert was a place of freedom and safety after the bondage of Egypt.

John's readers are expected to identify with the woman. The dragon's attack symbolizes the experiences of hardship, being at odds with the world, and, for some, arrest, punishment, and even execution. The identification of the dragon with Satan implies that their hardships are not meaningless, random events; rather they result from the struggle between good and evil. The rescue of the woman means that the struggles are not in vain. God will vindicate the faithful.

12:7-12—*The Dragon Thrown Down to the Earth*

The opposition in 12:7 is the opposition of verse 4 seen at a different depth of focus. The conflict between the two archangels, the good and the evil, is the conflict between Eve and the serpent, between her offspring and its offspring through the whole history of Israel, until the day when *the* offspring should come (Gal.3:16; 4:4). Then the child is born. His triumphant progress from nativity to ascension, unscathed by the dragon (for even his death is his own free choice), spells the dragon's defeat. From that time on, the people of the new Israel have been able to claim victory over the dragon, because of the Lamb's death and their witness to their own experience of its power. Even the death of the body no longer matters to them (12:11).

The "great dragon" is given his full title (12:9)—not in his honor, but as an expression of the prophet's exultation that the ancient foe had at last been overthrown. He is "that ancient serpent" of Genesis 3, where the serpent is but a guise for the devil, even as the dragon is in this chapter.

That Satan was "thrown down to the earth" (12:9) leads to an intensification of his activity on earth. Two things are in mind here: (1) That Satan has no place in heaven represents an important victory won for people, since Satan is no longer able to accuse people before God. This suggests that God will no longer listen to accusations against his people, for they are forgiven. (2) Satan's defeat in heaven signifies that his power has been broken in human affairs in history, so that even if he does intensify his efforts to control the nations and destroy the work of God, the extent of his influence is limited (he has for example no power over the church), and his days are numbered (12:13-17).

The central utterance of the song in 12:11 ("They have conquered him by the blood of the Lamb and by the word of their testimony") is the most significant statement in the chapter. It provides the real basis for the overthrow of Satan and the coming of the kingdom of God, as narrated in 12:9 and celebrated in 12:10. It also makes clear why there is no possibility of Satan lodging an accusation against the people of God. "The blood of the Lamb" has prevailed.

Through his glorification by God, earned by his earthly work and death, Jesus won a first and decisive victory (12:11) over Satan. Satan's power is thus basically broken; it is limited with regard to place (the earth, 12:9) and time ("his time is short," 12:12).

Satan's fight is not excited by any prospect of winning; he cannot win and he knows it. He is moved by the kind of despair that throws all plan and prudence to the wind, aware that he has nothing to lose (because he has lost it already).

12:13-17—The Dragon's Unsuccessful Persecution of the Woman

Verse 13 in effect tells us that in the face of his decisive, though not total, defeat in "heaven," Satan decides to do what damage he can to the church in the "little" time that he has.

Though warred upon, the woman will ultimately be kept safe (12:14). This is the same essential picture as 12:6 and parallels the sealing of God's people in 12:7 and the measuring of the temple in chapter 11. But chapter 12 clearly identifies Satan as the author of tribulation. This does not contradict the plague visions in which God was in some sense acting. Satan causes the tribulation, but even in his rebellion he serves God's ultimate purposes: to destroy evil and bring into existence the New Jerusalem.

In 12:16 we see that the "earth" to which Satan has come down (12:12) does not receive him, though her inhabitants do (13:4, 8). The "earth" is created by God and is good; Satan is derivative and destructive, a parody that is given reality by those who trust in him.

Summary

The two witnesses in chapter 11 represent the church. The three and one half years represent the whole time between Christ's first and second comings.

The sequence here with the witnesses (preaching, death, resurrection) is not a prediction of the coming chronological history of the church. It is rather a picture of the pattern of Jesus that we have seen earlier in Revelation—faithful life, suffering, death, resurrection, exaltation. This is also the pattern for those who would be Jesus' followers.

The seventh trumpet, in 11:15-19, brings us again to the end: "The kingdom of the world has become the kingdom of our Lord and of his Christ, and he shall reign for ever and ever." The end means the kingdom is fully come, all the faithful are rewarded, and the destroyers of the earth are themselves destroyed. In some sense the seal and the trumpet plagues have helped to bring this about. For all intents and purposes, we could now skip to chapter 21 and the vision of the New Jerusalem. The story has been told. But it is to be retold with added depth and meaning starting with 12:1.

Chapter 12 is a colorful recapitulation of what has been shown in chapters 6 to 11. The church is ultimately safe in the midst of persecution because of God's power and the blood of the Lamb. Its security is in safety from separation from God, not safety from physical suffering. The dragon could not quite devour the "male child" who was to rule. And the dragon could not and cannot destroy the church, although it tries.

Verse 6 speaks of the woman going into the desert for 1260 days (or three and one-half years). This is the place prepared for her by God. It expresses the same reality as the "sealing" of the 144,000 in 7:1-8 and the measuring of the temple in 11:1-2. All three juxtapose this with visions of suffering (here it is 12:11) indicating the promise of ultimate security with God no matter how bad things seem now, if only they remain faithful.

In 12:9 we are told that Satan is thrown down from heaven. This leads to an intensification of his activity on earth (cf., chapters 13-19). But John's readers are not to be deceived. As Satan is no longer in heaven he cannot accuse people before God since they are totally forgiven, due to Christ's work. Satan's ultimate power over human affairs is broken. The extent of his influence is limited and his days numbered.

What is new in chapter 12 is the first open identification of Satan as the author of tribulation. This does not contradict the plague visions where the Lamb is the one who opens the seals and the angels blow the trumpets. Satan does it, but God allows it and uses it.

Meditation

One of the central themes in chapter 12 is the struggle between the dragon (Satan) on the one hand and God, God's angels, and God's people on the other. The imagery is somewhat obscure, but that good and evil are struggling is clear.

The outcome of this struggle is not in question. The dragon is defeated:

> I heard a loud voice in heaven, saying, "Now the salvation and the power and the kingdom of our God and the authority of his Christ have come, for the accuser of our brethren has been thrown down, who accuses them day and night before our God. And they have conquered him by the blood of the Lamb and by the word of their testimony, for they loved not their lives even unto death." (12:10-11)

However, 12:17 indicates that in the face of his decisive, though not total, defeat in "heaven," Satan decides to do what damage he can to the church in the "little" time he has left before the final manifestation of the victory proclaimed in 12:10-11.

The book of Revelation as a whole provides some help for reflections on what characterizes the war made by Satan "on those who keep the commandments of God and bear testimony to Jesus" (12:17).

Satan "wars" against God's people mainly through the beast/Babylon/harlot figures. These manifestations of idolatry are all tied up with the sociopolitical order. They reflect the situation in society when immense pressure is used to gain support for the "powers that be" in order to maintain an unjust status quo.

That nonconformity is as much a threat today as it was in John's can be seen in the fate of various conscientious objectors, political dissidents, advocates of the poor, and others worldwide—in places like the United States, the Soviet Union, South Africa, Chile, and all too many others.

This pressure to conform carries the negative threat of persecution and suffering for nonconformists, for those whose understanding of God's truth leads them to say no to other proclaimers of absolute "truth." But it also carries a positive "threat"—the fruit of conformity (i.e., wealth, comfort, and blindness to God and God's concerns in the world).

We can see this illustrated in Revelation by comparing the description of the Laodicean church in 3:17 ("For you say, I am rich, I have prospered, and I need nothing; not knowing that you are wretched, pitiable, poor, blind, and naked") with that of Babylon in 18:7-8:

As she glorified herself and played the wanton, so give her a like measure of torment and mourning. Since in her heart she says, "A queen I sit, I am no widow, mourning I shall never see," so shall her plagues come in a single day, Pestilence and mourning and famine, and she shall be burned with fire; for mighty is the Lord God who judges her.

A person, a group of people, a society—all can grow overly self-confident and arrogant and thus lose touch with God and human reality . . . and suffer the consequences.

One can easily become blind to the way one is oppressing others. The jarring impact of 18:13, which lists various cargoes traded in Babylon closing with "and slaves, that is, human souls," would have surprised those in Roman society who did not see themselves trafficking in human souls in their conscience-free involvement in the Roman economy.

John saw himself writing in continuity with the Old Testament prophets and shared the perspective of Amos:

Hear this, you who trample upon the needy, and bring the poor of the land to an end, saying, "When will the new moon be over, that we may sell grain? And the sabbath, that we may offer wheat for sale, that we may make the ephah small and the shekel great, and deal deceitfully with false balances, that we may buy the poor for silver and the needy for a pair of sandals, and sell the refuse of the wheat?" . . . .
"On that day," says the Lord God, "I will make the sun go down at noon, and darken the earth in broad daylight. I will turn your feasts into mourning, and all your songs into lamentation; I will bring sackcloth upon all loins, and baldness on every head; I will make it like the mourning for an only son, and the end of it like a bitter day." (Amos 8:4-6, 9-10)

What is especially sobering about the situation in Amos is that the people being condemned were very religious and felt that their prosperity was due to their faithfulness to God, not realizing that it was instead the fruit of great injustice. If we still believe in the God of Amos, we cannot help but tremble when we realize that the poor of Amos's society have their counterparts worldwide today.

John's picture of the struggle with Satan emphasizes the dangers of nonconformity (persecution) and conformity (blindness). One of his central themes in the book as a whole is that a person who is truly following the Lamb need only fear the latter dangers. That is, ultimately we need only to fear the dangers of our turning away from God for the sake of social conformity.

The book as a whole contains many elements of a strategy for dealing with these dangers—elements for waging war against the dragon. In 12:11 the brethren conquered Satan "by the blood of the Lamb and by the word of their testimony." The effect of this was that "they loved not their lives even unto death." The battle against Satan is to be fought in the same way that Christ fought: through nonretaliatory love vindicated through resurrection.

This hope of vindication is what gives validity to the admonition to the Smyrnans in 2:10: "Do not fear what you are about to suffer. Behold, the devil is about to throw some of you into prison, that you may be tested, and for ten days you will have tribulation. Be faithful unto death, and I will give you the crown of life."

Jesus was the faithful witness (martyr). John argues throughout that those who will share Jesus' victory are those "who follow the Lamb wherever he goes" (14:4). The promise is vindication through faithful suffering and citizenship in a city where "God himself will be with them; [God] will wipe away every tear from their eyes, and death shall be no more, neither shall there be mourning nor crying nor pain any more, for the former things have passed away" (21:4).

Questions for Thought and Discussion

(1) Do you see the time between Christ's two comings as a time of "tribulation"? Why or why not? What evidence from human history, current events, and your own experience supports your view?

(2) Do you agree that "God sends no other agencies to people in the time of the earth's distress than the witness to Christ"? How is the church in general doing in this task? Your local church? You personally?

(3) What does 11:7 mean to you? What does the "beast" signify? Does this verse refer to past history, ongoing history, or future history? Does the beast have the upper hand versus God and God's people?

(4) Who do you think "those who dwell on the earth" are in the present day? Are you part of them? If not, what is your attitude toward them?

(5) How do you understand 11:15? What do you make of the present tense? Is there any way, in your view, that "the kingdom of the world *has* [already] become the kingdom of our Lord and of his Christ"?

(6) Who are the "destroyers of the earth" in 11:18? How do you think they are destroyed? Do we have any role to play in this? How can it be that this is a "constructive" thing (i.e., that good comes from it)?

(7) Can you relate to the woman's "pangs of birth" (12:2; cf. idea of Israel waiting for the Messiah) in your waiting for the "birth" of the New Jerusalem?

(8) What does it mean that "she brought forth a male child, one who is to rule all the nations with a rod of iron"? Do you understand this rod literally or metaphorically? If literally, why has this not happened? If metaphorically, to what does it refer?

(9) With regard to Revelation 12:3 and later references, what kind of power does the "dragon" (identified as Satan) have in the world? How should we relate to that?

(10) Assuming that 12:6 refers to God somehow protecting God's people in their time of tribulation, do you gain comfort and encouragement from that affirmation? Do you see it as a present-day reality?

(11) Do you derive any encouragement from the images in chapter 12 of the dragon being thrown from heaven to earth (12:9) and thus having no place in heaven from which to accuse people before God, and of the assertion that the dragon's wrath is expressed because "he knows that his time is short" (12:12)?

Revelation Thirteen and Fourteen
Spiritual Warfare, Part 2

Study Questions

(1) What new images are introduced in chapter 13? How are they related to each other? What ties does this chapter have with the preceding one?

(2) How would John's first readers have understood the imagery in chapter 13? Would such references as 13:3, 12, 15, 16-18 have been meaningful to them? Why?

(3) Does 14:1-5 recall earlier material in the book? How does this paragraph contrast with the material in chapter 13?

(4) What is the meaning of 14:13 in its context?

(5) What is the background and meaning of the imagery in 14:14-16? How is this imagery further elaborated by the additional element found in 14:17-20?

(6) Reflect on the larger movements of thought in the passage as a whole. What are the main themes? Is there movement toward a climax? If so, what is it? Does this passage have relevance for us today? How?

13:1-4—*The Awesome Beast*

The dragon's seven heads and ten horns (12:3) showed that power was of his very essence. Of all the attributes of God, omnipotence is what Satan likely would aspire most to have. The beasts of Daniel 7 are actually explained as being four great kings or empires. There also, power is of the essence. We are shown a beast whose power is not that of wealth or of influence, but of a government ("diadems" and a "throne") which combines all the powers of Daniel 7, and whose authority is worldwide (13:7). We see in the beast the principle of power politics—in a word, the state. For John this meant, of course, the Roman Empire. But every succeeding generation of Christian people knows some equivalent of it.

The beast's death and resurrection (13:3) may reflect the current widespread belief that the emperor Nero would return after death (if not in his own person, then in the person of one of his successors). But this "death and resurrection can also be seen in the realm of politics at any time in history (for example, communism, fascism, liberal democracy). The whole earth follows the beast with wonder (13:3), each one having seen how the head he idolizes can yet rise again. And all whose hope is not ultimately in the Lamb have no hope except in some human system, to which either expressly or by implication they give the blasphemous name of "god."

When one empire receives a mortal wound (i.e., is defeated and disappears), that is not the end of the beast. It simply continues on in a succeeding empire or kingdom or other political power structure. The wound that killed one empire heals, and the beast continues in power in another empire.

The beast called from the abyss by the dragon (Satan) in 13:2 is not government in and of itself. It is the *abuse* of it.

Only Christ's life and death could qualify as the "mortal wound," as chapter 12 has already told us. The wounded head, in the light of 12:17, refers primarily to God's words to the serpent that "her seed . . . shall bruise your head" (Gen. 3:15). The "beast," like the "great city" (11:8), personifies all opposition to God and his people from the beginning, and imitates the true Human's death and resurrection.

The "obedience" and "testimony" of Jesus and his saints

wound the beast's "head" (the word for "wound" here is the same as for "plague" in 11:6). Immorality and idolatry (as at Pergamum) and lack of witness (as at Laodicea) on the part of Christians restore its power to afflict them, and "the whole earth follows [it] with wonder" (contrast John 12:19). Worship of that which is "not God" releases demonic powers. Failure to maintain the "testimony of Jesus" is deadly not only to the church but to the world it is meant to save.

It was precisely Rome's demand that people render to Caesar and to the state that which belongs to God alone which compelled the early church to resist Rome to the death. John believed that in making this demand the state became demonic, and he vigorously represents this in 13:4 by drawing on ancient mythological pictures to caricature the role that the state and its rulers were playing.

It is said that "the dragon gave his power and his throne and great authority" (13:2) to the beast. But the dragon has been defeated and thrown out of heaven. Has he any authority to bestow on earth? Only insofar as the world is content to recognize his authority.

13:5-10—*The Beast's Limited Power*

The beast's power endures "for 42 months" (13:5), just as long as the time of the Gentiles (11:2), as long as the prophesying of the two witnesses (11:3), as long as the woman's abode in the wilderness (12:6, 14). In other words, the beast, in one form or another, will survive as long as the earthly duration of the church.

In 13:7 it is said that the beast "was allowed" to make war on the saints. This indicates that Revelation does not express a radical dualism. Yes, the beast rebels against God, but even that rebellion is part of God's plan. Creation may appear to be out of God's control, but even the persecution of the faithful is within God's providence. The suffering of the saints is unavoidable and is God's will. So the saying, "Here is a call for the endurance and faith of the saints" (13:10).

The beast is (for John) the Roman Empire, but its real threat to the church is not its sword, but its divine pretensions supported from within the church, which may lead Christians to take the wrong side when the final attack on the saints comes (13:7), and thus to expose them to a more deadly sword (2:12, 16). Likewise, the supreme disaster for the earth-dwellers is the Roman Empire which, as the inscriptions show, they take to be their supreme blessing. For it involves them in a love of darkness and hatred of the light which must bring a recoil worse than the scorpion's sting (9:5-6; 14:9-11).

"If any one has an ear let him hear" (13:9). In each of the seven letters to the churches these words accompanied the promise to the conqueror. By their solemn repetition here at the heart of the book John indicates that he is turning once again to give the church its marching orders. If God allows the monster to wage war on his people and to conquer them, what must God's people do? They must allow themselves to be conquered as their Lord has done, so that like their Lord they may win a victory not of this world.

In 13:9-10 John combines part of Jeremiah's oracle against Jerusalem (Jer. 15:2: "If anyone is to be taken captive . . .") with the saying of Jesus found in Matthew 26:52. The whole is a warning against any attempt on the part of the church to resist its persecutors. If Christians are condemned to exile, as John has been, they are not to lift their hands against the tyrant; to do so will be to deserve their punishment. It is precisely this suffering without resistance that calls for patient endurance and faith (cf., 1:9; 14:12).

What calls for patient endurance is that the church must submit without resistance to the attack of the monster. Only in this way can the monster be halted in its tracks. Evil is self-propagating.

13:11-18—*The Powerful Deception of the Beast from the Land*

Whereas the Lamb of God speaks the word of God (19:13 and chapters 2 and 3), the beast from the land (13:11) is the "lamb" of Satan, and it speaks the word of Satan. It looks "like a lamb" but its speech betrays its origins.

Verses 11-13 make clear what the beast from the earth is. Its looks are lamblike but its voice is dragonlike. It stands before the first beast, waiting on his bidding and ready to act at his command and speak with his authority. It is concerned with worship, the religious aspect of human life. It works miracles, like bringing fire from heaven (1 Kings 18). The coupling of Christlike appearance and Satanic message, the status of prophet, the concern with worship, and the appeal to the magical—all add up to one thing: false religion.

As a tool of Satan, "the deceiver of the whole world" (12:9)—the false prophet—deceives the inhabitants of the earth (13:13-15). The deception takes the form of emperor worship. They must "make an image for the beast": a reference to the images, set up in temples of Rome and of the empire to which divine honors were rendered.

By the deceiving messages of the false prophet (cf. 16:13; 19:20), the "image of the beast" (i.e., of the first beast, the "system") is presented as having a life of its own, apart from which people apparently cannot survive (13:15). And as the invisible seal of the Spirit confirms the divine ownership of God's servants (7:3), so the mystical mark of the beast confirms those who sell themselves to the "system."

The idea of the mark (13:16) is to provide a parallel with "the seal of the living God" (7:2), stamped on the foreheads of God's servants (7:1-8; the connection is explicit in 14:1). The seal of God marks out people as belonging to him, and so for preservation in his kingdom. The mark of the beast similarly identifies people as his servants, and without this mark they cannot live. The idea seems to reflect the practice in ancient society of marking people, by branding or tatooing, as the property of others, whether of slave owners or of gods.

The mark of the beast is symbolic of allegiance to Rome. Verse 17 implies that those without the mark were prevented from buying and selling. Roman coins generally bore the image and name of the current emperor. Refusal to use such coins severely inhibited one's ability to buy and sell in Asia Minor. Such a refusal by John and his first readers would not be surprising, since the emperor was often pictured as a god on coins. The Zealots, who rebelled against Rome in A.D. 66-70, refused to carry, look at, or manufacture coins bearing any sort of image. Their practice was based on a strict interpretation of the first commandment (cf. Exod. 20:4) and on the belief that the images and inscriptions of Roman coins were idolatrous. The vision here implies a similar judgment.

The number 666 (13:18) does not stand for any particular person or institution but simply for the beast. The church is symbolized by pictures (the elders, the woman, the two witnesses) and by a number (144,000). The church age is symbolized by pictures (the woman preserved, the witnesses preaching, the nations occupying Jerusalem) and by a number (three and one-half years). False religion is symbolized by a picture (the beast from the earth) and by a number (666). The number 666 does not mean Nero or Caligula or Rome. It simply means the beast, false religion.

The number 666 is eminently suitable to characterize the antichrist, since it implies a consistent falling short of the divine perfection suggested by 777.

Chapter 13 gives a parody of Christianity: a trinity (dragon, beast, false prophet), a death and resurrection, and a universal church with its sacrament of membership (13:16).

14:1-5—The Triumphant 144,000 with the Lamb on Mt. Zion

This passage is an important contrast to chapter 13. The picture there is only partial, the dominance of the beast only superficial. The real reality is here. Chapters 13 and 14 are essentially simultaneous. While the beast rages, those who are faithful stand strong in the midst of that. Their true fate is victory, not defeat. This is an important encouragement in the midst of tribulation and the dominance of the beast. "Hold on," John is saying. "In reality the Lamb is dominant, hidden as that may be now."

Some of the elements in the two chapters stand in contrast with each other. For instance, the persecuted Christians are no longer at the mercy of their enemies but stand triumphant "on Mt. Zion," the place of deliverance and divine glory (cf. Isa. 24:21-23; Mic. 4:6-7). They are in the presence of the true Lamb instead of the imitation lamb (13:11). They bear on their foreheads the "name" of the Lamb and his father's name instead of the mark of the beast. In reality, contrary to 13:3, not everyone did follow the beast. Some continued to follow the Lamb.

Verses 1-5 contain another reference to Psalm 2. Psalm 2:6 says, "I have set my king on Zion, my holy hill." But what John sees is not a warrior king but the Lamb. There is a good deal of battle imagery in the rest of Revelation, but ultimately no real battle is fought. The real battle is over with the events of chapter 5. What happens from now on is that the Lamb's soldiers conquer by the blood of the Lamb and by following the Lamb wherever he goes.

The 144,000 (14:1-3) represent the whole people of faith. As the 144,000 in chapter 7 had the seal of God on their foreheads (7:3), here they have the name of the Lamb and the father's name on their foreheads.

The redemption that the "new song" celebrates (14:3) is a mystery unfathomable to the people of this age (cf. 2 Cor. 2:6-9). It takes "faith" to be able to learn it.

In 14:3-4 the 144,000 are figuratively seen as male because they are "soldiers" of the Lamb. The Deuteronomic regulations for holy war are in mind here. They demanded that soldiers going to war preserve ceremonial purity (cf. Deut. 23:9-10). Ceremonial purity is maintained here by abstaining from illicit relations with the harlot Babylon (cf. 14:8).

"Following the Lamb wherever he goes" is a way of speaking about discipleship. These people are called the "first fruits for God and the Lamb" (14:4). They are the vehicle by which God means to move humanity toward the New Jerusalem. The church's experience should also be a sign of what the New Jerusalem will be when it fully arrives. The statement that "in their mouths no lie was found" (14:5) points condemningly to the lies of the antichrist.

14:6-7—The Gospel Proclaimed

The angel in 14:6-7 proclaims an "eternal gospel ... to those who dwell on the earth" (i.e., those who rebel against God, those who trust in the beast and dragon and worship them). These verses speak of the eternal gospel in broad, basic terms: Repent, trust in, and worship God as your Creator.

The emphasis here is the redemptive intent of God. The plagues are not just naked acts of judgment simply for the sake of punishment. They go hand-in-hand with offering the gospel.

In 8:13 an eagle flies in "midair" crying, "Woe, woe." Here in verses 6 and 7 the angel flies in "midair" crying, "Fear God and give him glory." Perhaps the two pictures are of the same thing. God's judgments are God's working to bring the end. This is woe to those who refuse God's offer of grace, but God's intent is always redemptive.

14:8—Babylon's Destruction Announced

Babylon must fall for the sake of her inhabitants. As long as people are drunk on her wine they will be deceived. If the source of the wine is cut off, perhaps people will see the light. God's work is to destroy the destroyer of the earth for the sake of the earth dwellers. So even if they lament Babylon's fall, it is for their own good. But some are so thoroughly seduced and "maddened" that they refuse to turn. They hold on to Babylon and thus go down with her.

Babylon is seen by most commentators to be a reference to Rome, but I see it as broader. Ancient Babylon was a rebellious civilization that tried to rule the world. It oppressed God's people, and was totally corrupted by the will-to-power. The term *Babylon* is used of a spiritual force that tempts all nations and has reared its head throughout history to a greater or lesser extent whenever nations have been imperialistic, utilized some sort of civil religion, or persecuted God's people.

Babylon falls. Revelation emphasizes that very strongly. But neither here nor anywhere else in the book is there any hint that she was attacked by outsiders. She collapses from within. She self-destructs.

14:9-11—The Importance of Loyalty to the Lamb

These verses emphasize one of the main points of this book as a whole. What is at stake now is people's loyalty. John is seeing beneath the surface and emphasizing that those who trust in the beast will suffer the consequences and those who trust in the Lamb will in the end be blessed.

These verses form a counter proclamation to the image of the beast in 13:14. There it was decreed that those who do not worship the image should be killed and those without the mark of the beast should be able neither to buy nor sell (13:15, 17). Here the angel pronounces a much worse fate for those who *do* worship the beast and bear his mark. They are to drink the wrath of God and endure eternal torment in fire and brimstone. This fierce warning is directed both to those that live on the earth and to those in the Christian community who might be tempted to deny their faith in view of the coming persecution.

In the Bible, God is seen as people's destiny—blessing for those who trust in God (Pss. 16:5; 23:5), ruin for those who do not (Ps. 75:8). It is not that God "gives" them ruin as such, but turning away from truth and embracing falsehood *is* ruin, which God *allows* to take effect. Babylon, the dragon, the beast, and the false prophet personify the effects of embracing falsehood—the self-destructive nature of sin and evil.

John is warning Christians to hold fast to the truth and not worship false gods. He is revealing the true nature and destiny of beast worship so that people in the churches might see and act now, before it is too late.

This angel brings the personal challenge: those who identify with the Babylon beast will share its fate, and also "drink the wine of God's wrath" (14:9-11). Those who identify with Christ will similarly share his destiny and endure to everlasting life (14:12-13).

14:12-13—The Reward for Loyalty

The speech of the angel here is addressed to the churches, not so that they may gloat over the retribution in store for the ungodly, but in order that they may prevent it from happening. The "patient endurance" that is called for is patient endurance in obeying God's commands so that those who live on earth might also come to know God.

The saying in 14:13, "Blessed are the dead who die in the Lord," is intended to strengthen the resolution of Christians facing the ultimate trial of strength with the antichrist. Death has lost its terror for the "dead who die in the Lord." They are united to him who by his death and resurrection conquered death for them. Their blessedness is rooted in the promise that their deeds will follow them.

14:14-16—The Harvest

Verse 14 relates to Christ's second coming. The reaping is for judgment in the widest sense. It is for gathering the righteous for the kingdom and the unrighteous for punishment.

This passage is unique in the Bible in speaking of the Son of Man as seated in a white cloud instead of the traditional storm cloud of Yahweh (cf. Ps. 18:9ff.). This may be intended to convey the thought of him coming in light and glory and blessing to a dark world. How we receive the "light" depends on our "eyesight" (i.e., whether we see with "eyes of faith").

The standard interpretation of these verses is that the grape harvest, which is destined for the winepress of God's wrath and produces a monstrous tide of blood, is the reaping of the wicked. The land will experience bloodbath from one end to the other.

However since is is outside the city (understood as the city of God), the city itself is kept pure. Within it there is no place for such defilement.

G. B. Caird in his commentary offers a different view. He looks back to the mention of "first fruits" in 14:4 with reference to the 144,000. They "follow the Lamb wherever he goes; these have been redeemed from among people as first fruits for God and the Lamb." This offering is being made in the grape harvest.

In 14:18 John speaks of the *vine*, a term never used in any of the Old Testament pictures of vintage judgment on the heathen. The vine was a traditional symbol for Israel. In the Gospel of John, *vine* is used of the New Israel (John 15:1-8). Therefore, here, too, the reference to the vine could lead us to infer that the gory vintage is used by John to portray the death of the faithful martyrs—the martyrs of the New Israel.

The punishment of Babylon comes when she is forced to drink the cup of God's anger. The winepress is not itself the punishment, but the place where the wine of God's wrath was being prepared. Before long John is to see Babylon "drunk with the blood of the saints and the blood of the martyrs [or witnesses] of Jesus" (17:6), and he is to hear a voice from heaven that says "mix a double draught for her in the cup she mixed" (18:6). Babylon's atrocities and God's retribution go together to make the double draught. From an earthly point of view, Babylon herself sheds the great river of blood by which the soil of her own territory is saturated and made drunk. But to the eyes of faith, the cup which will send Babylon reeling to her doom is being prepared in "the winepress of the fury of the wrath of God."

The place of the crucifixion was outside the city (14:20), so it was also the proper place for the martyrdom of those who held to the testimony of Jesus (cf. Heb. 13:12-13). Whatever element of judgment there is in the vintage, it is analogous to the judgment of the world achieved once and for all on the cross.

The implications of this interpretation are broader than one might think. The call here is for an all-encompassing disciplship, not just a literal martyrdom.

Summary

Chapter 13 pictures an "anti-Trinity." The dragon is anti-God, the beast from the sea is anti-Christ, and the beast from the land, the false prophet, is anti-Holy Spirit. Central in this chapter are the ideas of imitation and deception, and the spiritual nature of Satan's activities. These are not separate from the material world and social and political structures, but rather are infused in them. People's choices of where they work, how they spend their money, their political involvement—these are religious choices.

The first beast is pictured here in political terms ("thrones" and "diadems"). Rome is probably in mind, given the reality of emperor worship and persecution of Christians. But the beast's manifestations are not limited to the Roman Empire. The beast is active in any government that asks ultimate loyalty and is thereby worshiped.

The "obedience" and "testimony" of Jesus and his followers wound the beast's "head." Christians' immorality, idolatry, and lack of witness restore its power.

Verse 9 ('If any one has an ear, let him hear") refers back the seven letters and highlights the need to listen to and obey the command that follows. The call in 13:10 is for patient endurance and non-retaliation. The people of God are kept safe in the end if they reject the beast and refuse to become like the beast by fighting back.

The second beast (13:11) is called the false prophet and portrays false religion. The power of the dragon and the beast is deception. Their only power is the power that people give them. This beast is the "propagandist" (like Hitler's Goebbels). The "image of the beast" refers perhaps to emperor worship but more generally to whatever concrete thing is used to cause false worship.

The first five verses of chapter 14 stand in important contrast to chapter 13. If the purpose of chapter 13 is to show the true nature of Roman emperor worship and all other similar demands for ultimate loyalty made by the state since then (and the need for Christians to say no even if it means suffering and tribulation), then the purpose of 14:1-5 is to show the ultimate reality—that the Lamb is victorious and that those who follow him are also victorious. The beast's conquering (13:7) was only temporary and superficial. The faithful ones' real fate is that of singing on Mount Zion.

Verses 6 and 7 are intended to underscore the fact that God's purposes are redemptive. The hope that the plagues will bring about repentance is based not only on the fears that they will precipitate but also the continued, simultaneous offer of the gospel.

Verses 9-13 emphasize how crucial people's choices are. What is at stake during the "three and one half years" between Christ's first and second comings is people's loyalty. God has defeated Satan, but God wants no more than is absolutely necessary to meet Satan's destruction. We become like what we worship—the beast or the Lamb.

Verses 14-20 picture judgment. The grain harvest shows general judgment of the good and the evil. No one will escape. The grape harvest is a picture of the suffering of the faithful, whose blood will make up the double draught of wrath that will bring down the great harlot (18:6), who is another personification of the great anti-God city.

Babylon is guilty of shedding the blood, just like the rulers of this age were guilty of shedding Jesus' blood. These are the very acts that bring about that destruction.

Meditation

The central message of Revelation is that the Lamb of God has defeated the powers of evil, and that this act leads to the eventual destruction of all that opposes God. This affirmation arose in the midst of a practical awareness of the power of evil in the world. John and his readers were facing many tribulations on account of following Jesus. At the beginning of the book, John states that he shares with his readers "the suffering and kingdom and patient endurance that are ours in Jesus" (1:9 NIV). For him this included being exiled on the prison island of Patmos. In the letters to the seven churches we read of persecutions and martyrdom. Later on, we read more about martyrdom. Why was it that these Christians faced such difficulties?

The people of God have always been a threat to the "powers that be." This was true from the time of the Exodus when God liberated Israel from slavery in Egypt to the times of the prophets who called Israel back to the justice of God. It was the same in the time of Jesus, who came to preach good news to the poor and outcast and imprisoned and who practiced what he preached. There have always been people sensitive to God's call to not accept the values of the present age, the values of those who exploit the weak, and the private accumulation of power and wealth. These people have always been unpopular with the power structures upheld by these age-old values. This would most certainly have been the situation with the Christian in John's day. We can see this in the letters to the seven churches where the churches least troubled by persecution were the ones most at home with the world.

John and his readers faced a specific problem. It was not so different from the general tension between God's ways and the values of the old order, but of much more intensity. This problem had to do with hostility from the Roman Empire.

In the period of time shortly before Christ was born, a movement toward emperor worship arose within the Roman Empire. At the beginning it was more a worship of the empire than of a specific emperor. It was a grassroots development and had arisen because of the gratitude which people felt for the social order and stability afforded by the *Pax Romana* ("peace of Rome"). But because the emperor symbolized the empire and was more tangible, this worship soon focused on him.

In the beginning this new religion was at best tolerated by the emperors, who felt somewhat uneasy with being considered divine. But soon the social value of emperor religion became obvious. The Roman Empire included a large variety of nationalities, and the emperors saw common religion based on emperor worship as a helpful, even essential way to ensure unity within the empire.

With this religion you could keep your own religion also, but the bottom line was the confession that the emperor is lord. For Christians, there was never a question as to whether they could go along with this. Jesus was lord, not Caesar. Their commitment to integrity meant that they could not pretend to confess that Caesar was lord while still believing on the inside that Jesus was the only lord.

Because the Christians to refused to render worship to Caesar, they were seen as threats to the stability of the social order. This was not simply a religious issue; they were not simply heretics who did not believe the correct doctrine. Rather, they were dangerous rebels refusing loyalty to the emperor.

Perhaps we can see a similarity with young men who refuse to register for the draft today or who have resisted the draft in recent years. This is a problem to the state, but not primarily because the state needs the bodies of these specific young men. These kind of people would not make good soldiers anyhow. It is a problem because the young men refuse to give their ultimate loyalty to the state. They are threatening the social unity necessary for the state to maintain its power.

This call for emperor worship, the refusal of Christians to give it, and the resultant persecution and even martyrdom which resulted, provides the background for the visions John sees in Revelation 13.

The dragon spoken of here is labeled in Revelation 20:2 as "that ancient serpent, who is the Devil and Satan." What is described in chapter 13 symbolizes Satan's efforts to cause as much harm as he can on the earth in the time between his defeat at the resurrection of Christ (described in chapter 12 as his being thrown out of heaven) and his final destruction at the end of time.

To do this work, Satan has chosen as his agent two beasts. One comes out of the sea in 13:1 and the other comes out of the earth in 13:11. The description of these beasts contains a great deal of obscure imagery, but enough can be discerned to say that the first beast at least in part refers to the Roman Empire and the second beast represents emperor worship.

The first beast, the sea beast, uttered blasphemies against God, called upon all people to worship it, and made war against God's people. Authority was given to it over every tribe and people and tongue and nation. All these things were true of Rome. It called itself supreme and required total allegiance from its people. It had control over almost the whole known world and was persecuting the church during the latter part of the first century. Such was its power that people asked in wonder, "Who is like it, and who can stand against it?"

However, the people of God were told not to despair and above all not to retaliate. "If any one is to be taken captive, to captivity he goes; if any one slays with the sword, with the sword must he be slain. Here is a call for the endurance and faith of the saints" (13:10).

The real threat to God's people from the beast is not that they might be killed. The threat is that they might worship the beast. The real threat was not Rome's sword, but Rome's ideology.

John's vision, however, did not end with chapter 13 and the seemingly hopeless picture presented there. Despite the overwhelming power and authority which the beast possesses in chapter 13, John sees in the first five verses of chapter 14 the holder of the ultimate power of the universe. He sees a vision of the Lamb surrounded by his people, the 144,000—the whole people of God. This vision is a sign that God is still in control.

The relevance of this vision to John's readers was that the way to fight against the beast was, as 14:4 says, to "follow the Lamb wherever he goes." Chapter 5 tells us that the Lamb who was slain is the master of history. The Lamb who defeated evil through the way of love is the model.

According to these visions, there are two realities for the followers of the Lamb, both true at the same time. One reality is that of being warred upon by the beast and, at least in John's setting, being conquered by the beast. For John that meant being exiled to Patmos. For Jesus it meant being crucified. For others it meant martyrdom. But the other reality, and the one that is ultimate, is that of redemption—being at one with God, experiencing a sense of hope and security in the midst of tribulations and persecutions and evil.

John was writing to specific people facing specific problems. Clearly the problem here in mind is persecution from Rome and the demands Rome is making for Christians' allegiance. John is, in effect, calling upon his readers to remain strong, to have faith that Jesus' victory is real, and to hold fast to Jesus' way of love—the only way to deal with the beast.

Rome was only one manifestation of a spirit of cultural and political idolatry that has always existed and continues to exist. The term which is often used of the beast, though it never actually appears in Revelation, is "antichrist." This seems like an appropriate term since the beast is mimicking the Lamb and stands for the exact opposite of what Jesus stands for.

In relation to this passage, the antichrist should not be seen as a specific person such as Napoleon or the pope or Henry Kissinger. Rather, the antichrist is a spirit which is manifested every time people put their trust in values and institutions opposite of Jesus.

The spirit of antichrist is present when people's loyalties to idolatrous nationalism leads them to take the lives of their "enemies." It is present when people's commitments to prosperity and the American dream causes them to close their eyes to others literally starving around them. The spirit of antichrist is at work in our world. To the question, "Who is like the beast and who can stand against it?" our only answer is, like for John, "The Lamb who was slain."

We are called to follow him wherever he goes. Only in this way can we fight against the beast. A common term for this "fight" is the "Lamb's war." This "war" is fought with the weapons mentioned in Ephesians six: truth, justice, the gospel of peace, faith, and prayer.

In John's day, one clear test was whether they would worship the emperor. Our tests, perhaps, are not so clear. But we face them nevertheless. Our commitments to Jesus' way are continually tested. We are constantly tempted to give up hope, to think that evil is too powerful in our world. But John's vision reminds us that the Lamb is victorious. Let us follow his way.

Questions for Thought and Discussion

(1) How would you compare God's power and Satan's power? Is the difference only that one is stronger? Or are they different kinds of power? How can we discern which is which today? Can you think of examples? Or is everything too gray?

(2) Do you agree with this "political" reading of Revelation 13? Do the images here have any relevance in the present-day United States? How about the present-day Soviet Union? Present-day South Africa? Is it related to all countries, no countries, or some particularly evil countries? What are we told to do in response to the beast (cf. 13:10)?

(3) Do present-day governments demand that people render to Caesar and to the state that which belongs to God alone? What about (in the United States) war taxes? abortion taxes? education taxes? conscription? loyalty oaths? pledges of allegiance?

(4) Do you agree that the only authority the beast has to exercise on earth is that which people themselves give it? If that is so, what are the implications with regard to resisting that authority?

(5) How can the beast's rebellion be part of God's plan?

(6) Do you agree that the real threat of the beast to the church is

not its sword but its divine pretensions supported from within the church? What evidence is there for this in present-day North America?

(7) Why would John so strongly emphasize the need for Christians not to fight back against the beast (13:9-10)? What might this mean today?

(8) How does the false prophet deceive today? Where might you be especially vulnerable to its deception? What is the "mark of the beast" today?

(9) Can the song of 14:1-5 have any meaning for those not part of the conflict of chapter 13 out of which it arises? That is to say, if we do not know 13:7 can we know 14:5?

(10) What are the implications of "following the Lamb wherever he goes" (14:4) for resisting the beast's demands reflected in chapter 13? Does Jesus' example have any relevance for present-day political life (meaning our present-day relation to and involvement in our nation's political life)? If so, what? If not, why not and where else can we look for guidance?

(11) The idea of "first fruits" (14:4) implies election. Do you see yourself as part of God's firstfruits elected for the sake of moving humankind toward the New Jerusalem? If so, how does that affect your life?

(12) What might it mean to worship the beast (14:9-11) in our world today? What are the cutting edges in the present-day struggle between God and Satan for people's loyalty? Do you find the church (and yours in particular) a help or hindrance in this struggle? How could it help more?

(13) Do you share the sentiments of 14:13 with regard to the possibility of your own death? How is it that we can love life, hate death, and yet not fear death?

(14) Is it believable to you that suffering and martyrdom could be important means used by God to destroy evil? If so, does that belief affect how you live?

Revelation Fifteen and Sixteen
The Bowls

Study Questions

(1) How does chapter 15 prepare for the seven bowls?

(2) Compare the seals, trumpets, and bowls. How are they related in the whole scheme of the book?

(3) What is the meaning of the "sea of glass" (15:2)? Does the imagery occur elsewhere in the book?

(4) To what does the conquering of the beast refer (15:2)? Who are the persons who have conquered? Where? When? How? Does this contradict 13:7?

(5) Why should their song be called "the song of Moses . . . and the song of the Lamb" (15:3)? What emphases mark the content of the song?

(6) Give careful attention to the emptying of the seven bowls (chapter 16). What is associated with each bowl? Is any progression obvious? Any climax? What responses are indicated? How do these judgments compare with the two earlier series (seals and trumpets)? Does the imagery of these judgments recall any Old Testament material?

(7) How do the utterance of the angel and the response to it (16:5-7) compare with the song in 15:3-4?

(8) What figures do the symbols in 16:3 represent? How are they related to each other?

(9) What is meant by Armageddon (16:16)?

(10) What is the significance of the time element in 15:1, 8; 16:17? How is the statement "It is done!" (16:17) to be understood? How is it related to the remainder of the paragraph (16:17-21)? To what does Babylon refer (16:19)?

15:1-8—The End Continued

Again (15:1) we come *to* the end, but we still have more to see before the New Jerusalem comes down. The bowl plagues are said here to be the final outpouring of God's wrath.

Beside the sea (15:2) stood the faithful ones "who had conquered." This scene of the victors standing on the shore of the heavenly sea with harps in their hands praising God (15:2) recalls Israel's song of triumph over Egypt on the shore of the Red Sea. This scene is painted here as another message of encouragement and assurance of God's control and mercy. It significantly comes just prior to the last series of plagues to afflict humankind.

This vision also highlights the idea that the struggle against the beast is actually a struggle against paying homage to his image or being marked with the number of his name. Again, at stake here are people's loyalties and the continued faithfulness of the churches.

Like the Israelites after the crossing of the Red Sea (Exod. 15:1), the victors sang "the song of Moses, the servant of God" (15:3), celebrating the triumph of God over the enemies of his people. However, because the victory has been won by no other weapons than the cross of Christ and the faithful witness of his followers, this song is also the "song of the Lamb." The song holds out hope that the nations, in view of the just deeds of the Lord, will fear God and render God homage and worship (15:4). The promised result of God's just deeds here is that "all nations shall come and worship [before God]" (15:4). These same nations are ruled by the beast in 13:7 and rage at God's judgments in 11:18. The effect of God's justice is not to destroy them but to convert them.

In 15:5 the temple is viewed as the tabernacle that contains the testimony to God's abiding covenant and God's moral demand on humankind (cf. the Old Testament law). The plagues which are about to be described are in harmony with both aspects of God's holiness. They judge the rebelliousness of the earth and ultimately fulfill God's redemptive purpose for the earth.

The emptying of the bowls of God's wrath (15:7) is a standard symbol used by the prophets to represent God's judgments among people (cf. Ps. 75:8; Jer. 25:15ff.; 49:12ff.; Ezek. 23:33; Hab. 2:16).

The smoke that fills the temple (15:8) both reveals and hides the glory, awe, and mystery that surround God (Exod. 19:16-18; 40:34-38; 1 Kings 8:11; Isa. 6:4). Only when the seven plagues were poured out was it possible again to enter the temple. God's judgments remain a mystery until they have been executed. God's "strange work" with Assyria (Isa. 28:31, NIV) is a good example of this.

The clear implication of this passage in its context next to chapter 16 is that the plagues and outpouring of God's wrath are somehow part of God's justice. The references to the song of Moses and the Lamb serve to tie the plagues in with the Exodus and the Christ event. The ultimate effect and central manifestations of God's just deeds are salvific (i.e., the celebration of the conquerors and the worship of the nations focuses on the Lamb.) The conquerors celebrate because they have, by conquering the beast, contributed not to the destruction of the nations, but to their coming to worship God.

16:1-2—First Bowl: Boils

The first bowl plague is like the Egyptian plague of boils in Exodus 9:10-11. Just as the boils came on people and beasts in Egypt apart from the Hebrews, so these "foul and evil sores" afflicted only "the people who bore the mark of the beast and worshiped its image." The act of worshiping falsehood would itself seem to be as a severe a punishment as any could be.

16:3—Second Bowl: The Sea Turns to Blood

Bowl two concerns the sea, as did the second trumpet (8:9). There are many parallels between the bowls and the trumpets, but the bowls are final, the trumpets only partial. This is the final intensification of God's judgment—the last chance.

16:4-7—Third Bowl: Rivers and Springs Turn to Blood

Bowl three shows the springs and rivers becoming like blood. Perhaps this is a reference to Babylon shedding Christians' blood. But this action turns on itself. Babylon's water supply is destroyed by what she herself does. Evil destroys itself. That is how God's judgment works out.

God is called "just" twice here—first by the "angel of the waters," the one pouring out the bowl which turns the rivers and springs of water into blood; and then by the "altar," which apparently is a reference to 6:9-11, where John saw under the altar the souls of the martyrs who are crying out for God to avenge their blood.

The specific references to "justice" here have to do with God's judgment on those who "have shed the blood of God's saints and prophets (16:6). In this judgment God gives blood shedders blood to drink through the agency of the angel who turned drinking water into blood. This seems like a clear case of "eye for an eye" retributive justice. But there is more to it than that.

The plagues are clearly stated to be instruments of God's "wrath" (16:1). We saw earlier that the plague visions are John's attempt to show that God is at work in the midst of the evils and catastrophes endemic in human history. The powers of evil are used by God for God's own ultimate purposes—destroying the evil powers themselves and fully establishing the New Jerusalem.

The "wrath" in Revelation, while attributed to God, is the impersonal process *within* history of the process of evil being allowed. to destroy itself. Revelation contains numerous references and allusions to the "cup of wrath" (14:10, 19-20; 15:7; 18:6). The "cup of wrath" in the Old Testament is never used of what is to happen at the end of history. It always refers to certain specific events in history, either in the past or in the near future. Most of John's references to the wrath refer to the fall of Babylon, by which he meant the fall of the Roman Empire. This, he believed, was to be an event in future history, but not the last event. Nor was it to be an event brought about by direct divine action, but rather by the action of people in history—the kings from the East, in fact (cf. 17:16). To this event John applies the language of divine wrath. In so doing he is entirely in line with the Old Testament view of God's wrath in *not* treating the wrath as purely eschatological. On the contrary, it is fundamentally the working out in history of the consequences of human sin.

God's wrath here means that people reap what they sow, that evil rebounds on itself and is self-destructive. This process serves God's purposes in two ways—first by moving people to repentance due to their experience of the destructive consequences of their rejection of God; and second (according to John's visions) by culminating ultimately in the destruction of the evil powers and the establishment of the New Jerusalem on earth.

The theme of the first four bowls is that God's creation itself takes vengeance on those that do harm. The land, the sea, the fresh water, and the sun all play a part. The principle seems to be that "whereby a person sins, thereby he or she is punished." For example, the "mark of the beast" in 16:2 becomes ugly and painful sores—the symbol of its punishment. In 16:4-7, the ocean of "blood" which the worshipers of the beast have shed contaminates their own water supply. This image is picked up in chapter 17, where we see the harlot Babylon staggering to her appointed doom, drunk with the "blood of the saints and prophets."

The images in chapter 16 bear a striking resemblance to the plagues of the Exodus. All seven judgments here repeat in varied ways the plagues of Egypt. The first four verses of chapter 15 indicate that these plagues conclude in a redemption greater than that from Egypt. This promised redemption is the subject of a full-fledged vision in chapters 21 and 22.

In the context of the whole book, it would seem that there are four major purposes of the plague visions. One is to serve as a serious warning to Christians not to conform to the surrounding culture, not to accept the mark of the beast. A second is to promise that the evil events of history are not ultimately independent from God's purposes but in a mysterious way actually serve them. Third, in the context of the plagues John emphasizes that God is continually hoping for and seeking repentance on the part of those who dwell on the earth. A fourth purpose is to show that God's wrath, in hating and destroying evil, serves the purpose of cleansing creation so that in the new creation things will be whole.

This passage emphasizes that the outworking of "wrath" is part of God's justice. The implication is that evil has consequences, that it is self-destructive. The reality of God's wrath is necessary for evil to be destroyed, which is the only way creation can ultimately be liberated. God's wrath serves God's redemptive purposes.

16:8-9—Fourth Bowl: Scorching Heat

In both 16:9 and 16:11 (bowls four and five) there are references to the possibility of repentance. Even at this late point, nobody's fate is finally fixed. The purpose behind even these terrible bowls is to move people to change their ways so that they can be saved. None have to suffer these bowls if they choose not to. But it is possible to identify so completely with the beast that people continue, no matter what, to curse God.

16:10-11—Fifth Bowl: Darkness, Pain, and Chaos

The "throne of the beast" is Babylon, the city of rebellion against God. The picture here is of Satan invading the whole structure of society, as first planned by God, and perverting it to his own ends. The "world"—the organization of human society without reference to God—is the result. It is the satanic counterpart to God's society, the community of faith. Upon this the fifth bowl is poured and darkness and confusion result. When God's values are ignored, human society cannot function and it ultimately self-destructs.

16:12-16—Sixth Bowl: Evil Invasion from the East

The sixth bowl plague pictures, like the sixth trumpet (9:13-21), a terrible invasion from the east. This harkens both to Jewish and to Roman fears in order to underline the evil nature of the beast and the extreme danger he represents.

The frogs (16:13) were examples of unclean creatures. The beast, the dragon, and the false prophet all work together—a kind of "unholy trinity." This "unholy trinity" is clearly behind the "kings of the whole world" (16:14), who are assembled to battle God—definitely a statement about political power in the world.

Significantly, when we get to the battle in chapter 19, there is no battle. The rider on the white horse simply captures the beast and false prophet and throws them into the fiery lake. So what is going on here is, in a sense, a bluff. These armies do not have a chance. But they can deceive. People can think that they really do have ultimate power.

Hence the call to stay awake (16:15). In the face of the "greatness" of the kings of the earth, God's people must remain awake. Otherwise they are doomed.

Beatitudes were used by Jewish and Christian prophets both to embody proverbial wisdom and to support an emergency appeal. This latter usage would seem to be in mind here (16:15). Unlike a direct command (wake up), "blessed is the one who stays awake" is a call for the readers to examine themselves (Am I awake?).

The origin and precise meaning of the term "Armageddon" (16:16) is unclear. Most likely it refers not to a specific place as much as to an event.

16:17-21—Seventh Bowl: The End

This final plague is of cosmic range, so the seventh angel poured his bowl "into the air." This plague sweeps away time and history. Everything that has been constructed out of rebellion against God is destroyed.

The great city (16:19) is obviously Babylon (i.e., Rome). The catastrophe that John is seeing is a social and political catastrophe, not a natural one (as in 6:12-17). Afterwards, its victims are still there to blaspheme (16:21) and the onlookers are still there to lament (18:9-18). And the final judgment is still to come (20:6, 11).

Summary

Chapter 15 presents another picture of the people of God—safe, victorious, and worshiping the Lamb. This comes as a word of reassurance prior to the great bowl judgments of chapters 16 to 18. They have "been victorious over the beast and his image," a dramatic reversal over 13:7 where it is said that the beast conquered them. By following the pattern of Jesus, they defeated the beast even as the beast apparently defeated them.

The picture in 15:4 of all nations coming to worship God is also an important one prior to the plague judgments. God's purpose is to destroy the destroyer of the earth for the sake of the nations. God is not seeking to destroy those who follow the beast, but only the beast itself.

Chapter 16 pictures the bowl plagues—the final and total judgments. They have much in common with the earlier seals and trumpets, especially the trumpets. The main difference is their intensification. The seals pictured one-quarter destruction, the trumpets one-third. Here it is total. The connection between the three is not chronological (first one happens in history, then the next, and finally the bowl series), but rather is logical. God warns us in the midst of these tribulations. As people resist, the plagues intensify. If they/we continue resisting, it will ultimately be too late.

The purpose of the plague visions is fourfold: (1) to warn Christians who were tempted to conform to their evil social environment, (2) to promise that the evil pictured here is not ultimately independent from God's pruposes, (3) to indicate that God longs for repentance and that as long as history continues God seeks repentance, and (4) to show that God's wrath serves the purpose of cleansing creation of evil.

Bowls five through seven, like seal six and trumpets five and six, picture a social-political catastrophe, not a natural one. Even after the seventh and last bowl, its victims are still there to blaspheme God (16:21) and the onlookers to lament (18:9-18). Everything is not literally destroyed. But God has pulled the rug out from under so-called civilization totally and decisively. The destroyer of the earth is finally totally destroyed and we are almost ready for the New Jerusalem to come down. But first, we will look more closely at the seventh trumpet in chapters 17 to 19 and then at the ceremonious judgment of good and evil in chapters 19 to 20.

Meditation

Chapters 15 and 16 are notable in the book of Revelation for their emphasis on God's justice. "Just" is a key term used in Revelation to describe God's work. Why is God "just" in Revelation?

It is John's intention to show that everything in human history is somehow used by God for the purpose of establishing the New Jerusalem. All of God's "just deeds" are ultimately redemptive—for creation, for the faithful witnesses, and ultimately for the nations and the kings of the earth (cf. 21:24).

It is Jacques Ellul's conclusion in *Apocalypse* (New York: Seabury, 1977) that justice in Revelation is consistent with the evangelical image of the justice of God which is the parables of the worker at the eleventh hour, and the lost sheep, and the pearl of great price, and the prodigal son, and the unfaithful steward—such is the justice of God. Neither retributive nor distributive. It is the justice of love itself, who cannot see the one he judges except through his love, and who is always able to find in that fallen miserable being the last tiny particle, invisible to any other than his love, and which he is going to gather up and save (pp. 212-213).

There are indeed visions of destruction in Revelation (chapters 6 to 20), but they are bracketed by the overarching vision of God as Creator and Redeemer (chapters 4 to 5)—the one who makes all things new (chapters 21 to 22). Thus the carnage and chaos are within God's plan and culminate in the fulfillment of human destiny in final union with God.

This final redemptive product of God's just deeds is not simply a collection of individuals. John believed in a purpose for collective human history as well as for individual souls. Into the New Jerusalem are brought not only the souls of the faithful but the wealth and glory of the nations. Down the middle of the city's streets are avenues of the trees of life, whose leaves provide healing for the nations. Every righteous achievement of people in the old order, however imperfect, will find its place in the healed and transfigured life of the New Jerusalem.

As in Exodus, so also in Revelation, the crucial event is not the plagues. Those do not exemplify God's justice but only serve the true end of God's justice: the redemption that leads to the new world.

The fulcrum of Revelation is not Jesus' return and the descent of the city of God described in the closing visions. Rather it is the vision of God and the Lamb in chapters 4 and 5. The slain and risen Lamb pictured there has accomplished redemption. He has risen to the throne of God and has begun his reign with God. The turn of the ages lies in the past. The clearest and most decisive expression of God's justice in the Christ event.

The Lamb in chapter 5 is also identified as the ruling Lion of the tribe of Judah. The Lamb that is slain is at the same time the bearer of seven horns (the symbol of complete power) and the seven spirits of God (the symbol of the fullness of the Holy Spirit). Revelation proclaims the paradox that the suffering and dying Christ is the victor.

John sees Jesus Christ as both the Redeemer and the Judge— not one after the other, but one because of the other. In two passages (14:14-20; 19:11-16) there is indeed a picture of judgment, but it is the judgment of the cross. Its intention not to tell us that Christ and the saints will sometime in the future conquer and judge their enemies, but to tell us that by virtue of the victory won once for all on the Cross, Jesus and his faithful followers "are more than conquerors," and that this applies to all post-incarnational history.

That Christ's past historical death and resurrection are central is seen in the fact that the visions of Revelation never show him engaged in direct battle with the dragon. Nowhere does John mention such a battle, not even in the portrayal of Christ's coming in 19:11-21. Christ has won his battle only as the Lamb who dies for the world (5:5, 9; 3:21). Therefore, according to the interpretive hymn of 12:10-12, humankind's possibility of victory over the dragon is found only "by the blood of the Lamb," that is, in the death of Jesus for them and "by the word of their testimony," whose content is the victory promised by the Lamb's death.

This centrality of the Lamb in Revelation leads to a reversal of conventional wisdom regarding power and justice. The power of love is true justice. If the lamb reigns over history, it is not as a crowned king, like Caesar, but as the incarnation of love itself, the love which goes so far as to give itself, to abandon itself. His power is none other than the power of this kind of love.

The book of Revelation affirms that God's just deeds accomplish the destruction of the evil powers which imprison humankind. John clearly differentiates between these powers, who are God's real enemies, and human beings, for whose sake these powers must be destroyed.

A power of evil beyond the sinful wills of individuals (personified in Revelation by entities such as the beast, the dragon, the false prophet, and the harlot) is seen to be at work in the processes of history. It is destructive of all that is good in this world, and it exceeds the wit or strength of humankind to overcome it. Just as Christ by his redemptive deeds delivers from sin and brings the powers of the coming age into this world, so too, Christ alone can bring the struggle between the powers of good and evil for ultimate sovereignty over creation to its final conclusion.

It is perhaps here that John's apocalyptic imagination is the most creative and profound. His visions show a procession of plagues (most if not all of which reflect natural and social catastrophes endemic in all eras of human history). Even after the worst of these plagues, human beings remain on the scene (cf. 16:21; 18:9-19). The culmination of the plagues is the destruction of Babylon (chapter 18) and the casting of the dragon, beast, and false prophet into the lake of fire (20:10). After this, John reports a vision of the New Jerusalem, where by the light of the glory of God "the nations walk; and the kings of the earth shall bring their glory into it" (21:24).

The goal of the "just deeds" of God, according to the overall message of Revelation, is not the punishment and destruction of people but rather the destruction of the destroyers of people.

Discipleship is not directly discussed much in Revelation, but it is nevertheless an important concern of John's. A central aspect of this concern is the repeated exhortation to Christians to remain "pure," to not conform to the society around them. Revelation speaks not only of judgment against the dehumanizing anti-God powers but also warns Christians not to give in to these powers' very concrete pressures. The book therefore begins with the seven letters, which form a section of censure and challenge to faithfulness. The injunctions, beatitudes, warnings, and promises which run through the book continue this function.

The only way that the followers of the Lamb participate in the battle versus the evil powers is to remain faithful throughout their lives. In that way they will conquer. This participation that Christians are called to in Revelation is, however, seen to be quite important. The church has been appointed by Christ to be a "kingdom of priests" (1:6; 5:10)—to mediate his royal and priestly authority to the whole world. Through the church the Lamb is to exercise his authority over the nations (1:5; 2:26f.; 11:15ff.; 12:5; 15:3-4; 17:14; 19:11ff.). Through the church he is to mediate God's forgiveness and lead the world to repentance (3:7-9; 11:13; 14:6-7; 20:1-6). And all this Christians may achieve only by following the Lamb wherever he goes (14:4).

This means that the separation of the church from the world is thought of more in moral terms than physical. Christians are called upon to refrain from moral and spiritual impurity while acting as agents of God's justice, maintaining "the testimony of Jesus," and validating it with their lives in "the street of the great city." It is by their own "just deeds" (*dikaiōmata*, 19:8) that Christians bear witness to God's "just deeds" (*dikaiōmata*, 15:4).

The essential thrust of the message of Revelation regarding justice is that justice ultimately has more to do with concepts like correction, reconciliation, and restoration of relationships than with concepts like retribution and an "eye for an eye." Like most of the rest of the Bible, Revelation strongly challenges any tendency to separate God's love from God's justice. God's "just deeds" in Revelation serve God's loving intention of making the New Jerusalem a reality. By doing so, they decisively bring about the healing of the nations (cf. 22:2).

It follows from this that a Christian concern for justice should always take a redemptive slant. Certainly injustice must be opposed, but never in a way that contradicts the dictates of love and reconciliation. Revelation 21 and 22 imply that the only way that the kings of the earth could make it into the New Jerusalem was to be converted (cf. 21:27). They did not make it as oppressors and worshipers of the beast. But the hope is that even they can be converted. They are not objectified as "enemies" and then disposed of.

In this perspective, "justice" is redefined to a certain extent—in the sense that it is considered with a different attitude and with different goals. Justice in Revelation is still concerned with brokenness in the world, scarcity, violation of moral norms, distribution of goods and services, and the like. But how I or someone else can get my or his or her due, how our self-interests can be balanced, how we can maintain a moral equilibrium in the world, how the punishment can fit the crime, etc.—these are not the questions of Revelation's justice.

How the values of God's kingdom can be incarnated in the human order, how social brokenness can be corrected for the good of all concerned, how enemies can be reconciled, how victim and offender can experience healing—these are Revelation's questions of justice. Here it is recognized that something will be missing from the New Jerusalem if it is not also accessible to the kings of the earth (should they somehow be freed from the snares of the beast).

Revelation asserts that the short-term result of the saints' "just deeds" would be their suffering. Jesus' just deeds resulted in his death. The implication of this is that a Christian perspective on justice cannot expect to be rationally acceptable to everyone in the world (a criterion seemingly axiomatic for modern-day philosophical ethics). The message of Revelation points toward a perspective on justice which challenges Christians to justice as care for the outcasts and other needy, love of enemies, and self-sacrifice to the point of martyrdom—a perspective based on the Christ event.

The theology of Revelation includes the affirmation that the way of the Lamb and his faithful followers is best for human society—indeed for all of creation. The book includes an implicit criticism of the worship of coercive power as ultimately satanic and idolatrous and thus totally self-defeating.

If this theology is at all true, then it would follow that the most socially "responsible" thing Christians can do would be to practice the Lamb's justice in every way possible. Revelation promises that such practices will likely lead Christians to share in Jesus' fate of martyrdom. It is not reading too much into history to assert that that promise has often been fulfilled and continues to be, daily, in our time. But Revelation also promises that the ultimate fate of Jesus—resurrection and exaltation—is also the fate of those who follow his way.

Questions for Thought and Discussion

(1) What is the basis for the affirmation in 15:2 that God's people have "conquered the beast"? Does their "success" have implications for our struggles versus modern-day "beasts"?

(2) What do you make of the connection in 15:3 of the song of Moses and the song of the Lamb? Is John making a statement of the unity regarding redemption in the Old Testament and in the New? Do you see unity or contradiction? What can *we* learn from the "song of Moses" (i.e., the Exodus event)?

(3) Why are God's deeds called "just" (15:3)? Does this kind of justice have anything to say to contemporary human strivings for justice?

(4) Do you agree that the connection between these three series

of plagues (seals, trumpets, bowls) is not chronological but logical? How does one's answer to this question affect one's interpretation of the book as a whole?

(5) 16:7 alludes back to 6:9-11. How do you understand God's answer to the prayer in 6:9-11? Is this picture consistent with your view of God and God's love for humankind? Why or why not?

(6) Do people "curse" God (cf. 16:9, 11) today? Why do they? What is your attitude toward them?

(7) What might characterize people today who are faithful to the exhortation in 16:15? How seriously do you take the warning in that verse?

(8) Do you see God warning us in the midst of present-day personal and social tribulations? If so, what is God warning us about and what kind of response is appropriate?

Revelation Seventeen and Eighteen

The Fall of Babylon

Study Questions

(1) What could be the writer's expectation with the invitation issued in 17:1-2?

(2) What imagery is employed in 17:1-6 and with what meaning? What dominant suggestions does the vision of the woman give?

(3) Note how 17:8-14 interprets 17:7. How do you understand the interpretation? What additional detail is supplied by 17:15-18?

(4) In the interpretation, what is the relation between the beast, the heads, and the horns?

(5) What does the angel's expectation of 17:15-18 add to the whole?

(6) In chapter 18, who are the participants and what role does each play? To what or whom does Babylon refer?

(7) What is the dominant tone of chapter 18? How is the tone produced? What introduces a note of conflict? With what effect?

(8) How is the greatness of Babylon portrayed? How is the sinfulness presented? How is the completeness of Babylon's fall conveyed?

17:1-6—*Summons to View Babylon's Punishment*

Chapters 17 and 18 elaborate the seventh bowl. Verse 19 of chapter 16 says, "The great city was split into three parts, and the cities of the nations fell, and God remembered great Babylon, to make her drain the cup of the fury of his wrath." In his picture of Babylon, John is issuing a sharp warning to those in the church who might be allured by her. That is his primary concern.

John is summoned to view the judgment of the harlot by one of the bowl angels (17:1), who also later (21:9) appears to show John the bride, the wife of the Lamb—the New Jerusalem. The contrast is crucially important. When the great harlot is seen to be who she actually is, the bride also will be seen to be who *she* actually is— in all her beauty and true wealth.

Cities counted as Israel's enemies are occasionally called harlots by the Old Testament prophets, for example Nahum 3:4 regarding Ninevah; Isaiah 23:17 regarding Tyre. When the Jewish people were in rebellion against God this image was used of Jerusalem (Isa. 1:21; Jer. 3; Ezek. 16; 23).

The adultery into which the harlot seduces the inhabitants of the earth and their kings (17:2) is not mere sexual sin; it is the worship of the dragon instead of God (cf. 13:11-12).

John is carried away in the Spirit to the desert (17:3). This is a place of safety and refuge (cf. ch.12), a secure place from which to watch what happens. Only there could he be safe from the lies of the dragon, the threats of the beast, and the seductions of the harlot.

The "scarlet beast" here is of the same type as the dragon (who was red—12:3) and the beast from the sea (who had ten horns and seven heads, each with a blasphemous name—13:1), but it is not identical with them. The blasphemous names that cover its body indicate that it is corrupt through and through. Perhaps some reference is meant to the blasphemous claims to deity made by Roman emperors who used such titles as "divine," "savior," and "lord."

The golden cup the harlot held was filled with "abominations" (17:4). They are not so horrible in terms of conventional morality. But the *idolatry* was a horror—an abomination. Abomination was a characteristic Jewish term for an idol.

Verse 5 explicitly identifies the harlot as Babylon. Rome is in mind, but as a representative of the spiritual reality of rebellious human civilization. Babylon is also other empires: ancient Assyria, France under Napoleon, imperial England, Germany under Hitler, the present-day United States and Soviet Union. The concern is with people's loyalties and commitments.

"The woman [is] drunk with the blood of the saints" (17:6). This is the wine of God's wrath which causes her downfall.

17:7-14—*The Corrupt Kings Exposed*

This section has caused as much, if not more, speculation than the earlier references to "666" and "Armageddon." The "seven kings" may refer to the history of "human kingship" or political authority. That five have already fallen is a sign that the end is nearing. We only have "three and one-half years" to go. That the beast is an eighth king but belongs to the seven could indicate that he is the real power behind their power.

The main point in these verses is that the kings are corrupt; they are deceived by the harlot, and are opposed to God. People of faith must not worship them, but must stay with the Lamb. Verse 14 affirms again the victory of the Lamb.

17:15-18—*Evil's Self-Destruction*

Verses 16 and 17 contain a fascinating image. The beast turns on the harlot and brings her to ruin. This is a vivid symbol for the self-destructive nature of evil. It turns on itself and destroys itself. God is behind it all somehow, directing what happens and using the beast's fury "until the words of God shall be fulfilled." This is the kind of thing that happens throughout the book. The deeds are done by evil beings, not by God. But God uses them.

18:1-3—*"Fallen Is Babylon the Great!"*

In 18:1 the earth which is made bright from the splendor of the angel is an allusion to Ezekiel 43:2, which speaks of God's splendor making the earth bright. Ezekiel used this to highlight the destruction of Jerusalem and to connect it with the promise of a new Jerusalem. John's use of the image may be similar. It is a sign connecting the judgment and destruction of Babylon with the coming of the New Jerusalem.

The angel's speech in 18:2-3 is in the form of a funeral dirge—a song of mourning. The reference to Babylon's fall alludes to a number of Old Testament passages, the most significant being Isaiah 13:19-22:

> Babylon, the glory of kingdoms ... will be like Sodom and Gomorrah when God overthrew them. It will never be inhabited or dwelt in for all generations; ... wild beasts will lie down there, and its houses will be full of howling creatures...."

The root image is total destruction.

Some people understand *Babylon* as referring strictly to Rome. Others see it as a broader, more universal symbol of which Rome was but one example. The connection between Babylon and Rome was made by contemporary Jewish and Christian writers (cf. 2 Baruch 11:1; Sybilline Oracles 5:143, 158; 2 Esdras 2; 1 Peter 5:13). But Babylon embraces more than one culture or empire and should be seen in terms of dominant ideologies more than geographical or temporal boundaries. Certainly this critique of Babylon was originally primarily a critique of Rome. But it applies to any society characterized by similar realities.

Verse 3 alludes to Jeremiah 51:7: "Babylon was a golden cup in the Lord's hand, making all the earth drunken; the nations drank her wine, therefore the nations went mad." The image of all the nations drinking "the wine of her impure passion" implies complicity. Perhaps Babylon was deceptive, but all the nations willfully joined in. "Fornication" implies idolatry, spiriutal bondage, and total compromise.

This verse reflects a strong antipathy on John's part toward the "powers that be" in the empire, both at the center (Rome) and at the outskirts (the nations like Asia Minor). These outskirts were part of the empire and their leaders willingly joined in Rome's practices and values. The early mention of the merchants, who are highlighted more than the kings of the earth in this chapter, indicates that John had a special concern for the unjust economic impact of Roman rule and commerce.

These verses set the tone for the rest of the chapter. They reflect a negative view of Rome and of the complicity of local leaders in

Roman dominance and injustice. We also found here a special concern about economic exploitation and an implicit warning to John's readers regarding the dangers of compromise and, ultimately, of idolatry.

18:4-8—The Call to "Come Out of Her"

Verse 4 is a key verse. The call, "Come out of her, my people" echoes numerous calls in Isaiah and Jeremiah to the people of God in Babylon. It may also allude to the calls concerning Sodom and Egypt (cf. Rev. 11:8). If so, the call picks up the Exodus motif, applying it to the movement from Babylon to the New Jerusalem.

In reference to ancient Babylon, Jeremiah 51:6 proclaims in strictly negative terms, "Flee from the midst of Babylon, let every person save his life! Be not cut off in her punishment, for this is the time of the Lord's vengeance, the requital he is rendering her." Isaiah 48:20 had a more positive emphasis: "Go forth from Babylon, flee from Chaldea, declare this with a shout of joy, proclaim it, send it forth to the end of the earth; say, 'The Lord has redeemed his servant Jacob!' "

This call to "come out" should be seen as metaphorical. It calls its hearers to refuse to cooperate with Babylon's injustice, idolatry, and violence. But it is not a call to physically remove oneself from the Roman Empire, for chapter 11 includes an implicit call for the people of God to witness on the streets of the "great city."

Verse 4 also reinforces the motif of the "eschatological protection" of God's people. They will not be a part of God's ultimate destruction of the forces of evil. The call here is similar to the sealing of the 144,000 in chapter 7 and the measuring of the true worshipers in 11:1-2. It announces the eschatological protection of those who remained faithful at the great day of the Lord. The image of Babylon's sins piled high as heaven in 18:5 underscores her evil by identifying her with ancient Babylon (cf. Jer. 51:9 where Babylon's "judgment has reached up to heaven and has been lifted up even to the skies"), the tower of Babel (Gen. 11:4), and perhaps even Sodom (Gen. 18:20-21).

Babylon gets her just deserts, 18:6 tells us. The implication here is that Rome is to be destroyed just as she herself destroyed. She had waged many wars to gain control over others and had destroyed

Jerusalem in A.D. 70. The idea of the double draught can be traced back to Jeremiah's preaching regarding Judah's judgment: Yahweh "will doubly recompense their iniquity and their sin, because they have polluted the land with the carcasses of their detestable idols,and have filled God's inheritance with their abominations" (Jer. 16:18).

Babylon is to be judged for her self-glorification and luxuriating (18:7). She is ambitious and totally self-absorbed and therefore blind to her own injustice and oppression.

Verse 7 contains one of the more striking images in the chapter. Babylon deserves judgment because of her complacency and arrogance: "A queen I sit, I am no widow, mourning I shall never see." This closely parallels Isaiah 47:5-9:

> You [Babylon] shall be called the mistress of kingdoms.... You said, "I shall be mistress for ever." ... Now therefore hear this, you lover of pleasures, who sit securely, who say in your heart, "I am, and there is no one besides me; I shall not sit as a widow or know the loss of children": These two things shall come to you in a moment, in one day; the loss of children and widowhood shall come upon you in full measure, in spite of your many sorceries and the great power of your enchantments.

The widow was the perfect example of poverty and helplessness— the opposite of Rome's splendor and power. But John is echoing Isaiah's proclamation that in a moment she will lose everything. An ironic contrast to this impending widowhood is pictured in Revelation 19 with the marriage supper of the Lamb.

According to Leviticus 21:9, the punishment of harlotry was to be "burned with fire." One background prophecy to John's vision in 18:8 is Ezekiel 23:25-35 conerning Jerusalem, which concludes, "Because you have forgotten the Lord and cast him behind your back, therefore bear the consequences of your lewdness and harlotry." Images like this suggest that John was not making a strict church/ world separation as much as he was a separation on the basis of coherence with God's values. When the faith community departs from these values it, too, receives judgment. And the works of the nations which cohere to these values will find their way into the New Jerusalem.

The emphasis on the suddenness of the judgment in 18:8 underlines the urgency of the call to "come out from her" in 18:4 and the foolishness of Babylon believing her own claims in 18:7.

18:9-19—A Taunting Dirge

The special source behind this section is the prophecy of the fall of the great Phoenician shipping city of Tyre in Ezekiel 26—27. Tyre was especially blameworthy in Ezekiel's eyes because it gloated over the fall of Jerusalem (26:2), possibly because Tyre could gain some economic advantage thereby.

This section, a litany of sorrow utilizing the dirge form, makes up the core of the chapter. Within the section, the lament of the merchants (18:11-17) is central, being flanked by the kings' lament (18:9-10) and the shipmasters' lament (18:17-19).

The effect of this structure is to focus attention on the merchants and their grieving at the loss of so much wealth (18:17). This loss was due to the greed of the merchants in contributing to Babylon's wantonness. They consequently were going down with her in her judgment. Perhaps to some degree John reflects an antipathy toward merchants characteristic in general of premodern societies.

John highlights the merchants in this chapter for a number of reasons. First, he was aware of and likely agreed with the Old Testament prophets' negative views of foreign trade, which facilitated ties with foreign nations. Besides the risk that such a contact brought in itself, foreign trade brought wealth, heightened social stratification, and oppression of the poor.

Second, John was concerned with temptations facing Christians living in commercial centers like Thyatira and Laodicea. The church at Thyatira was taken to task for tolerating the cultural conformist tendencies of "Jezebel" (2:18-29), and the church at Laodicea deceived itself into thinking (falsely) that because of its material wealth it was in need of nothing.

A third reason John focused on the merchants stemmed from his perspective that wealth tends to create a false sense of security (cf. the harlot in 18:7) which blinds people, preventing them from seeing greed, cruelty, and injustice in their true light.

The use of the dirge in articulating the laments of the kings, merchants, and shipmasters evokes sense of sadness, poignancy, even awe over such a loss. "What city was like the great city?" (18:18) in the mouths of the shipmasters echoes John's feelings. Back in chapter 17 he had to be told to not stare in wonder at the great harlot (18:6-7).

John, however, is aware of the city's true nature. The jarring conclusion to the list of cargoes in 18:12-13 emphasizes this. The cargoes are listed in descending order of value, finishing with livestock, "horses and chariots, and *slaves*, that is *human souls*"!

John's purpose in this passage was not to evoke sympathy for Babylon and her cohorts. Kings, merchants, and shipmasters, mournful as they were, were not people John's readers would have empathized with. The ultimate purpose of the songs of lament was to announce in one more way the judgment—subtly yet effectively.

18:20-24—Call to Rejoice at Babylon's Demise

Verse 20 also precludes sympathy for Babylon with its call to rejoice over the fall. The point is not to gloat, but be grateful. Such gratitude and rejoicing could instill faith in a time when Babylon seemed anything but fallen.

The literal sense of 18:20b is "God has judged her for the way she judged you"; that is, as Babylon has (unjustly) found the saints, prophets, and apostles guilty and condemned them, so God has done the same to Babylon. John likely had the law of malicious witness in mind here; "If a malicious witness . . . accuses his brother falsely, then you shall do to him as he had meant to do to his brother" (Deut. 19:16-20).

John alludes to various Old Testament passages in this section, perhaps the central one being Jeremiah 51:60-64, which concludes: "When you finish reading this book [of Babylon's evils], bind a stone to it, and cast it into the midst of the Euphrates, and say, 'Thus shall Babylon sink, to rise no more, because of the evil that I am bringing upon her.'"

Key phrases in 18:21-24 (NIV) include "never to be found again" and its variants "never be heard again" and "never shine . . . again." These are used first of Babylon herself, then of the various mundane, human things which will no longer be found in her: musicians, craftsmen, the sound of a millstone, the light of a lamp, the voice of bridegroom and bride. This refrain is then given an ironic and very telling twist in 18:24: "And in her *was found* the blood of . . . all who have been slain on earth." This is the final and perhaps most forceful reason given for Babylon's condemnation, effectively emphasized as the conclusion of the vision that makes up chapter 18.

The "mighty angel" John reports on in 18:21 is the third mentioned in the book. The other two had to do with the two scrolls (5:2; 10:1) which contain the records of God's work in fulfilling God's purposes in history. The reference to the mighty angel here likely implies that with the final fall of Babylon, those purposes are fulfilled.

The merchants are brought into the picture again in 18:23 as perhaps the prime example of how "all nations were deceived by the harlot's sorcery." The harlot controlled the lives of the people who grew rich from serving her.

The black arts were common in John's world, but the reference here to "sorcery" would seem to be broader. John likely had in mind Rome's apparent control of the world's powers and resources; the perception of which led people to accept her claims to divinity and eternality. In particular, the "sorcery" is put in direct relation to commerce and wealth. This certainly could be an echo of Jesus' teaching regarding the dangers of wealth.

The concluding reference to Babylon proclaims that "in her was found the blood of prophets and saints, and of all who have been slain on earth." Besides emphasizing a major reason for Babylon's condemnation, this comment serves to universalize Babylon beyond just Rome. Babylon somehow encompasses every society that has unjustly shed the blood of righteous people.

This closing section, like 18:9-19, evokes sadness, poignancy, and a sense of tragedy. But the punchline of 18:24 effectively precludes any sympathy for Babylon and her fate.

Summary

Chapters 17 and 18 elaborate on the seventh bowl (16:19), emphasizing that Babylon—the "anti-Jerusalem," or city symbolizing human civilization in rebellion against God—will not escape judgment.

Babylon, the great harlot, is pictured as it really is: corrupt, evil, deceptive, and seductive. This is a blunt statement meant to warn

Christians to avoid Babylon's enticements because they lead only to death. Rome and the idolatry of emperor worship may have been in mind, but the warning applies to all manifestations of the spirit of Babylon.

In the midst of the discussion of Babylon, John reminds his readers of the victory of the Lamb (17:14) and of the fact that the Lamb is the true King of kings and Lord of lords.

Verses 16 and 17 of chapter 17 show the beast turning on the harlot and bringing her to ruin. This is a vivid symbol for the self-destructive nature of evil. It turns on itself and destroys itself. God is behind it all somehow, directing what happens and using the beast's fury for God's purposes until "God's words are fulfilled."

Chapter 18 is a lament over Babylon's fall modeled after Ezekiel's lament over Tyre (Ezek. 26—28). Babylon was a place for people with many good, human activities that were at times twisted and corrupted. Unfortunately, much of what could have been good was corrupted.

God's people are called to "come out of her" (18:4). Wake up, do not be deceived, if you take part in her sins you are bound to share in her plagues.

The kings, merchants, and sea captains do not go down with her. They stand afar off and lament her fall because they cannot continue their worship of her. But now, perhaps, with the great deceiver gone they may wake up and turn back to God.

Meditation

The fate of two cities dominates the last six chapters of the book of Revelation. These two cities are Babylon and Jerusalem. It is surely no coincidence that John discusses what happens to both in the same context. John is providing a picture of the destiny of the city dedicated to opposing God. He shows the city of death and the city of life.

While we see clearly here the contrast between the two cities, we nonetheless must not lose track of the fact that the things that happen to them, their ultimate fates, are all part of *one* work of God, the work of bringing about salvation for people of every tribe and nation.

God's work of destroying evil is portrayed in Revelation as three series of seven plagues each. Each series is more intense than the one preceding it. The first series—pictured as the opening of the seven seals attached to the scroll in chapter 6—shows one quarter of the earth being killed. The second series of plagues is portrayed as seven trumpet blasts in chapter 8. The vision of the trumpet plagues shows one third of the earth being burned.

The third series of plagues is portrayed in chapter 16 as seven bowls being poured out. The effect of the bowl plagues is total. Whereas in the trumpet plagues we are told that one-third of the living creatures died (8:9), with the bowl plagues we are told the "*every* living thing died" (16:3).

These various plague visions are awesome and terrible. It is important to remember that they are symbolic. Even after all the plagues, which if taken literally would seem to have killed every person in the world many times over, we still read of people cursing God (16:21).

The plague visions represent the spiritual battle taking place between God and the forces of evil. But it is a special kind of battle. The outcome is already decided, due to the victory of the Lamb who defeated death by his nonretaliatory, unconquerable love. This means that evil will indeed be destroyed, that the New Jerusalem will replace Babylon as the habitat for those who dwell on the earth.

Although the victory has actually already been won, the battle still continues for a time. What is at stake is the loyalty of the people on earth. Satan, the dragon, maintains the power to deceive, to receive worship and trust. The victory of God is experienced by people in this age as the ability to remain faithful to the way of the Lamb and to worship nothing else.

The wrath of God is worked out as evil is exposed for what it really is. It turns on itself and eventually destroys itself. This process is pictured in chapter 17, where we are told that the beast itself brings the city of Babylon to ruin. "For God has put it into their hearts to carry out his purpose" (17:17).

God's purpose is the total redemption of creation. The end result of this work of redemption is the destruction of Babylon—the symbol of all that is opposed to God's love—and the establishment of the New Jerusalem: "The dwelling of God is with people. He will dwell with them, and they shall be his people, and God himself will be with them and be their God; he will wipe away every tear from their eyes, and death shall be no more, neither shall there be mourning nor crying nor pain any more, for the former things have passed away" (21:3-4).

Historical Babylon was a city-state in what is now southern Iraq. It gained prominence as an early empire dominating other city-states in the time around 1700 B.C. To maintain its political control of the Middle East, Babylon imposed its religion and its worship of the god Marduk on the whole area. Babylon thus became a kind of holy city.

In the seventh century B.C., after a time of decline, Babylonia regained its control of the area. This included domination of Israel. Babylon then became the symbol for the anti-God forces in the world. It was a combination of their oppressive political dominance and their pagan religion that made the Babylonians so evil in the sight of the Israelite prophets.

The real Babylon rapidly lost its importance. It was conquered by the Persians in 539 B.C. and gradually lost its power and prestige. By 100 B.C. it was pretty much forgotten and by A.D. 200 it was totally deserted. But the *idea* of Babylon—as a theological symbol—remained very strong among the Jewish people. In later Jewish writings after the Old Testament and the New Testament, Babylon was the clear symbol of the anti-God forces in the world. Babylon is therefore used in Revelation as a symbol for the concentration of forces of evil, the forces which oppose God and God's way of love.

On one level, Rome is being thought of here. As the historic Babylon had oppressed God's people and tried to impose a false religion on them, so too Rome oppressed God's people and tried to impose the false religion of emperor worship. It would thus stand to reason that Rome would be called Babylon. That Rome was not supreme or immortal—that Rome's oppression of them would someday end—is an important affirmation for John and his readers.

It would be wrong, however, to tie this image too closely to Rome, or to any other literal city. That which is destroyed in chapter 18 is not people, but spiritual forces. The kings of the earth, the merchants, the sea captains—all of whom were corrupted by Babylon—stand and watch Babylon get wiped out. But they themselves are not wiped out.

This shows that the real enemies of God are not people. Rather, the enemies of God are the great harlot, Babylon (who bewitches all the nations), the dragon, the beast, and the false prophet. These are all symbols of the spiritual reality of evil which God must destroy for people to be truly free and able to fulfill God's creative intentions.

These enemies of God have corrupted the whole earth. They have corrupted the kings of the earth, who have transformed the necessary function of providing for social order into one of providing wealth and privilege for themselves and their special interest allies. These kings are themselves victims of the harlot Babylon, in whom they trust and who fails them.

These enemies have also corrupted the merchants of the earth, who have misused valuable and worthwhile resources, part of God's good creation (18:11-13). These merchants are totally obsessed with their own wealth, even to the point of being indifferent to the buying and selling of their bodies and souls of human beings (18:13). These victimizers are also themselves victims of the magic spell of the harlot. Ultimately, their quest for wealth leaves them with only poverty. When Babylon falls they experience only terror.

It is essential to realize that it is for the very sake of the kings and merchants and captains that Babylon is destroyed. Ultimately, the magic of evil can only be broken when evil itself is destroyed. When that happens, the fruits of creation are no longer worshiped themselves, but will be given their proper place in God's order. These same kings of the earth who mourn the fall of Babylon will in the end bring their splendor into the New Jerusalem (21:24) along with the glory and honor of the nations (21:26).

Again, the enemies of God are not people but rather the forces which destroy that which is human in people—the forces which cause people to rebel against God and do violence to other people. People are to be loved. This is the idea behind Jesus' call for us to love our enemies and Paul's call for us to pray for our persecutors.

The proper response to violence is not only concern for the victim and anger at the evil which has been done, but also compassion and love for the oppressor. Persons who surrender to Satan and use violence separate themselves from God and dehumanize themselves in that act, even as they dehumanize our victims. The oppressor, too, falls victim to the evil powers.

True healing, true redemption, comes only when the cycle of evil is broken, when the hate of the oppressor is countered by love. A story I read recently illustrates this idea. Will Campbell is a Southern Baptist preacher who has for many years been active in civil rights work in the South. In his book *Brother to a Dragonfly* (New York: Seabury, 1976), Campbell tells how in the mid-1960s he was at a meeting of Northern student activists where they were shown a CBS documentary film on the Klu Klux Klan. The film documented such horrors as the murder of three civil rights workers and the death of four Sunday School children in Birmingham. Viewers were then taken inside a Georgia Klan hall where an initiation ceremony was in progress. At one point the candidates were lined up in military formation and the command, "Left face!" was shouted. One scared and pathetic figure turned right, bringing confusion to the formation and cheers, jeers, and catcalls from the audience viewing the film.

Campbell concluded that there were no true radicals in that whole audience. For if they were radical, how could they laugh at a poor ignorant farmer who did not know his left hand from his right? If they had been radical, they would have been weeping, asking what had produced him.

The people who serve the forces of evil are themselves victims of those very same forces. God's destruction of Babylon is for the benefit of those who served the harlot as much as it is for the benefit of the prophets and saints whose blood was found there (18:24).

Our call, in the light of this, is to love our enemies, to seek their redemption—for that is how we are seen to be children of God.

Questions for Thought and Discussion

(1) What does Babylon refer to? Does it have a present-day manifestation? Why do you or do you not think so?

(2) Do you agree that in his condemnatory picture of the harlot, Babylon, John is in reality issuing a sharp warning to those in the church who might be allured by her? What might be alluring about the Babylon of John's day? How about the Babylons of our day? How can we help one another resist this allurement?

(3) In terms of your own awareness and life experience, what do you think the most important contrasts between Babylon and the New Jerusalem are?

(4) Do you think that the image of a harlot could be applied to the church in history and/or the present? Is this label irrevocable?

(5) Are there "blasphemous names" (17:3) in use today?

(6) Do you agree that Babylon is Rome but also ancient Assyria, France under Napoleon, imperial England, Germany under Hitler, the Soviet Union, and the United States? Why or why not?

(7) Can you think of examples of how evil turns on itself? Do you think God is behind this phenomenon?

(8) What is the point of the social criticism of Babylon (Rome, et al.) in chapter 18? Is it merely condemnatory or meant to motivate John's readers to faithfulness and good deeds?

(9) Do you think 18:9-19 is a criticism of wealth and commerce? Are there any valid reasons for focusing on the merchants as the special mourners of Babylon's fall? Might these still apply?

(10) Does it make any sense to you to say that the fate of Babylon is part of God's redemptive work in establishing the New Jerusalem?

(11) Do you agree that we should make a distinction between the forces of evil at work in people and the people themselves? If so, how does that affect your attitude toward people in the world? Do you want *your* enemies to be freed from Satan's hold? Does one's view of these things affect one's understanding of how violent Revelation is to humans? How can we say that it is for the sake of the kings and merchants that Babylon is destroyed? Is that possibly true yet today?

Revelation 19 and 20

The Final Triumph

Study Questions

(1) What two suppers are contrasted in chapter 19 (See Ezek.38—39 and Luke 14)?

(2) What does the symbolism of "the marriage supper of the Lamb" convey?

(3) Does 19:8 suggest salvation by works? What is the meaning of 19:10b?

(4) Note the description of Christ in 19:11-16. What is the significance of the various symbols associated with him? How does this description compare with others in the book? What is the mission of the rider on the white horse? Compare with the first seal.

(5) What is the significance of 19:21 as a clue to interpretation?

(6) What is your understanding of the millennium? What other biblical parallels to the 1000 years of chapter 20 are there?

(7) What disposition is made of the trinity of evil? On whose authority? What becomes of their followers?

(8) Only at 20:11 is God's throne described as "white." Is the color symbolism important? What is the meaning of 20:11b?

(9) Who is judged and by what standards? Is salvation finally determined by works?

(10) What is the meaning of 20:14?

(11) What is the relation between the martyr, the rest of the dead, and the first resurrection?

(12) What does the great white throne add to the consummation of the judgment of God?

19:1-10—A Roar of Exultation

Following the account of the destruction of Babylon in chapter 18, John envisions a scene of great celebration. God's judgments are said to be "true and just," for God, "has condemned the great prostitute who corrupted the earth by her adulteries. God has avenged on her the blood of God's servants" (19:2, NIV).

These true and just judgments lead directly to the wedding of the Lamb in 19:7, which is the real focus of the celebration. The wedding marks the reign of the Lord God Almighty (19:6). The bride, which symbolizes the followers of the Lamb, is said to have made herself ready by putting on the fine linen given to her to wear. The linen "stands for the righteous acts of the saints" (19:8, NIV).

Salvation is being celebrated in this passage. This means that all that has stood in the way of God's rule has been removed. (See the account in chapters 17 and 18 and the ultimate effect of the plague series, along with the visions in 19:11-21 and chapter 20.) It also means the New Jerusalem can now come down.

The affirmation that God's sentences are "true and just" recalls the altar in 16:7, to the song of Moses and the Lamb in 15:3, and to the announcement of judgment in 11:18. Salvation, glory, and power belong to God. These are political terms and gain significance when seen in the political context of John's day. The Emperor Augustus had been called "savior of the Greeks and of the whole inhabited world," "savior and benefactor," "savior and founder," and "savior and god." His birthday was called the beginning of "good tidings" (gospel). He was known as the "just and generous lord" whose reign promised peace and happiness, (i.e., salvation). The heavenly choir John saw was therefore asserting that not Caesar's but God's power and salvation that is revealed in the justice given out to Babylon/Rome and its cohorts.

The real celebration here is for the destruction of Babylon as one element of the coming of God's reign and the marriage of the

Lamb. The references to justice here: (1) tie together God's justice, the destruction of the evil powers, and ultimate salvation; and (2) emphasize the importance of the Lamb's followers doing deeds of justice.

19:11-16—*The Victor on a White Horse*

This is another vision of judgment, telling the story again from a different angle. Jesus is clearly the one who carries out God's wrath here.

It is important to try to interpret this passage consistently with what we know about Jesus already. He does not suddenly completely change character, coming first as a suffering servant and then as a vicious, all-powerful warrior judge.

The white horse that Jesus is riding (19:11) symbolizes victory. He comes as the one who has conquered sin, death, and evil through his death and resurrection. As the following verses make clear, he comes to this apparent battle with the forces of the antichrist *already* the victor. This battle was foreseen in 16:13-14 ("three foul spirits that look like frogs . . . go abroad to the kings of the whole world, to assemble them for battle on the great day of God the Almighty"). The outcome of the battle in no way is in question.

The rider is called "Faithful and True"; that is, "the faithful and true witness" of 1:5 and 3:14. He is the one who remained faithful and true to God even when it meant a martyr's death. That is how he gained the white horse.

The "war" he wages is the war between good and evil, and it is won by remaining faithful to the way of the cross in the face of temptations to follow other ways.

"On his head are many crowns" (19:12, NIV); perhaps in contrast to the dragon's seven crowns (12:3) and the beast's ten (13:1). He is the true King of kings and Lord of lords. The name no one but himself knows is perhaps a reference to the fact that Jesus transcends all human understanding.

Verse 13 contains a key image. The rider approaches this battle "clad in a robe dipped in blood." The blood has already been shed *before* the battle begins. This is an allusion to Jesus' blood shed on the cross and is the reason why no real battle takes place here. He can already ride the white horse because the real battle is over, and he won it on the basis of his shed blood.

The "armies of heaven" (19:14) likely are the saints wearing their bridal linen (19:7-8). They carry no weapons, for they, too, are already victorious.

The only weapon mentioned at all is the sword that comes out of Jesus' mouth—his word, the gospel (cf. Heb. 4:12; Eph. 6:17). This is what ultimately brings the nations to their knees.

The "wine press of the fury of the wrath of God" (19:15) could, in the light of the grape harvest in 14:17-20, be a reference to the means by which the wine which brought down Babylon is prepared. Babylon was brought down by the wine of martyrdom—the martyrdom of Jesus and the saints. The suggestion here is that God is causing this wine to take effect.

The "great supper of God" (19:17-18) is the same as the "marriage supper of the Lamb" (19:9). It is the time of judgment; for those who belong it is a time of great rejoicing, for those who do not it is a time of condemnation (cf. Jesus' parable of the supper in Matt. 22 where the one without wedding clothes on is kicked out).

The birds eating the flesh of all people (19:18) represents an act of judgment. This is in line with the interpretation that the angel in midair preaching the gospel in 14:6 is the same thing as the eagle in midair in 8:13 calling out "Woe!" This judgment reveals the true status of people. Either they are with God or against God. It is clear here that the battle has already been decided.

The beast and the kings and armies are all ready for battle (19:19). They truly are deceived to think that one will occur. The battle is long past. Jesus simply captures the beast and false prophet and throws them into the fiery lake (19:20). There is no battle.

"The rest of them" (19:21, NIV)—those who were deceived by the false prophet—are now judged by the word of Jesus. The birds ate their flesh. With the deceiver gone, maybe they have some hope of seeing the light. Verse 24 of chapter 21 indicates that the kings of the earth bring their splendor into the New Jerusalem.

John is convinced that Jesus—in his death and resurrection—won the only battle necessary to defeat evil. Picturing him in another battle would imply that his first victory was not good enough. Christ's victory in this passage is simply the revelation of the one sufficient victory he has already won.

20:1-3—Satan Bound for the Thousand Years

The focus of 20:1-10 is on the fate of the dragon, Satan. In chapter 19 we saw what happened to the beast and the false prophet. Here we turn to the power behind their power. These verses retell what already happened in chapter 19, but from a different perspective (a common technique in Revelation). Thus, the millennium is *not* here a future, literal 1000-year period of time but is rather another symbol for the time between Christ's first and second comings.

In 20:1-3 a nameless angel is enough to seize the dragon and bind him. Once Satan is cast out of heaven through the work of Jesus Christ (cf. chapter 12), he has no effective power against God at all.

Background to this picture is Jesus' reference in Luke 11:21 to binding the "strong man," which illustrated what happened to Satan with Jesus' first coming. When Jesus cast out evil spirits, he demonstrated that Satan, for all his strength, had been seized and bound.

Satan's binding symbolizes his limited ability to act and especially his lack of power to do anything ultimate to the saints. Verse 11 of chapter 12 tells us that the saints have conquered him by the blood of the Lamb. Satan is bound for the same length of time that the faithful witnesses reign with Christ (20:4), symbolizing his impotence against them.

The 1000 years is a difficult number to interpret. I understand 1000 to symbolize a large number—one too large for humans to count. (The idea of a literal millennium is not mentioned elsewhere in the Bible.) Some have thought it significant that one day is like 1000 years to God (Ps. 90:4; 2 Pet. 3:8). The 1000 years may seem like a long time to people, but to God it is only a day and God's work will be shortly done.

20:4-6—The First Resurrection

Verses 4 through 6 treat the reward to the faithful witnesses. This is another version of several earlier visions: the multitude in white robes rejoicing in 7:9-17, the rejoicing at the casting out of the dragon from heaven in 12:9-12, the worship of the 144,000 on Mt. Zion with the Lamb in 14:1-5, the promise of the blessedness of those who die in the Lord in 14:13, the victorious ones singing the song of Moses and of the Lamb in 15:2-4, and the time of the wedding supper of the Lamb in 19:9. The point is that here and now God's people reign as kings and priests, as 1:6 affirms.

The "first resurrection" may refer to what is described elsewhere in the New Testament as a passing from death to life; that is, a person's rebirth as a Christian (cf. John 5:24; Eph. 2:5; 1 John 5:11-12). These people are all who trust in Christ and follow him alone as Lord. They have no fear of the "second death" (the final judgment).

The point of these verses is that what seems to be defeat, persecution, even literal death, for the sake of Jesus, is really a victory. Those who resist the beast, who oppose its will to power without being corrupted by it, will share in the first resurrection and truly reign with Christ and truly be priests.

This is, again, a very strong word of encouragement to John's readers to hold fast to the way of Jesus and the way of real power.

20:7-10—Satan's Doom

These verses retell the vision of 19:11-21 in briefer form, focusing on the dragon. Satan is "released" not so he can actually make war against the saints, but so that he will take himself to his own destruction. His being released is analogous to the intensification of the plagues in the last plague series, the bowls. Evil finally is exposed and destroyed.

The names "Gog and Magog" come from Ezekiel 38 and refer to human nations in rebellion against God. They are essentially the same as Babylon. It is an obscure reference. The point of it is to highlight the reality that the nations are in rebellion and that God's victory is complete and total.

Verses 8 and 9 say the same thing as 19:17-21. Here: "Their [the rebellious nations] number is like the sand of the sea. And they marched up over the broad earth and surrounded the camp of the saints and the beloved city; but fire came down from heaven and consumed them, and the devil who had deceived them was thrown into the lake of fire and sulphur." In 19:19 the "kings of the earth with their armies gathered to make war against him who sits upon the horse and against his army." But the beast and the false prophet, who had deluded the nations, are captured and thrown into the lake of burning sulphur (19:20). The armies in 19:21 are killed with the rider's sword and their flesh eaten by birds; in 20:9 they are devoured by fire from above. The imagery is similar. It is judgment imagery, and it reveals the true desires of their hearts.

The fate of the dragon in 20:1-10 is similar to that of the beast earlier. As Satan here is bound, released, and destroyed, so the beast in chapter 13 is killed, then comes back to life, and finally in chapter 19 is destroyed.

20:11-15—*The Great White Throne Judgment*

There is one more matter to be dealt with before the New Jerusalem comes down: the great white throne judgment.

Note the main points here are. *First, everyone,* great and small, is brought to account for the lives they lived; no one escapes the judgment of God.

Second, people are judged according to what they have *done,* not just what they believe. This picture supports Jesus' teaching about the centrality of discipleship. John is saying to his readers, "How you live matters!" The "book of life" records those who have true faith. Faith and works go together. Faith without works is dead, but there are truly no good works without faith.

Third this judgment is real. It *will* come. And it comes prior to the New Jerusalem, for there will be nothing unclean found there.

Fourth, Death and Hades are finally thrown into the lake of burning sulfur. They have no more power over people once those who are in the book of life are reunited with God and those who are not, meet their final fate in the lake of burning sulfur. In Paul's words, "The last enemy to be destroyed is death . . . [then] God may be all in all" (1 Cor. 15:26, 28).

Summary

In 19:1-8 we see a grand picture of worship in heaven. The worship has been inspired by God's justice which has destroyed evil and brought to pass the wedding supper of the Lamb. Both are necessary for the new Jerusalem to come and God's promise of salvation to be fulfilled.

In 19:11 Jesus comes onto the scene as God's warrior-judge. But the war is over, for all intents and purposes, due to his victory in the cross. What we see here is not a battle but simply the carrying out of God's judgment. The beast and false prophet are thrown into the lake of fire. "All the rest" (those who were deceived) are judged by the word of Christ (the sword comes out of his mouth).

Jesus, dressed in a robe stained with his own shed blood, is pictured here as the true ruler. He is so powerful that he simply throws his enemies into the lake of fire—without resistance. This vision powerfully supports John's continued call to his readers to remain faithful to the way of Jesus and to resist worshiping the dragon and beast and harlot.

In short, 20:1-10 retells chapter 19 with a different focus, centering on the fate of Satan. Verses 1-3 describe his binding, emphasizing the time between Christ's two comings, and the binding of Satan with his limited ability to act during this time (i.e., he cannot separate God's people from God's love). The recurring interlude of God's people rejoicing (7:9-17; 12:9-12; 14:1-5; 14:13; 15:2-4; 19:9) is taken up again in 20:4-6. They can rejoice because seeming defeat—martyrdom for the sake of Jesus—is really victory in God's sight.

Satan is released in 20:7-10 so that he can take himself to his own destruction. Like the beast in 19:17-21, the dragon leads the rebellious nations against God but is summarily taken and thrown into the lake of fire with no battle being fought. This again highlights the real battle having occurred with Jesus' cross and resurrection.

The great white throne judgment (20:11-15) is for *everyone* on the basis of what they have *done*. It culminates in the final destruction of Death and Hades. In Paul's words, "the last enemy to be destroyed is death. . . . [then] God may be all in all" (I Cor. 15:26, 28).

Meditation

In chapters 19 and 20, especially 19:11-20, John gives us several "reruns." He uses battle imagery to present a picture of Jesus Christ winning the ultimate battle in the conflict between good and evil. Jesus does not do this through a bloodbath; rather, it has already been accomplished in the past historical event of his death and resurrection.

John's view of the last things (eschatology) is totally determined by his view of the decisiveness of Jesus' past victory over the powers of evil. In 1:5 he speaks of Jesus as the "ruler of the kings on earth" *in the present.* He *has* "made us a kingdom" (1:6). John hears Jesus assert "I died, and behold I am alive for evermore, and I have the keys of Death and Hades" (1:18).

The key passage in the whole book is chapter 5. An important point this passage makes is that "the Lion of the tribe of Judah, the Root of David, *has* conquered." This Lion, of course, is none other than the slain Lamb, Jesus of Nazareth. The efficacy of this "conquering" is seen in chapter 19. Though the forces of evil are gathered for battle, Jesus and his angels simply capture them without even fighting. The real battle is long past.

The dragon has already been defeated. Thus we can learn from the history of the Lamb *how* to play our role in effecting this victory. And we can do this in the hope that the ultimate power in the universe is God's suffering love.

As we have seen in looking at the plagues in Revelation, Jesus' resurrection did not bring an end to history. His victory is yet to be completed. Revelation looks *forward* to a last day in which the New Jerusalem comes down and heaven and earth are one. John's "realized eschatology," however, sees the *crucial* event as past, meaning that that event determines what future events will look like.

Jesus' life, death, and resurrection also determine the shape of our task as his followers. There is a sense in which the Lamb's war continues in our world and will continue until the last day. It is important that we have hope in that day. But it is equally important that we recognize our present responsibility to live (and fight) in the light of both the past event and the future event.

We learn from the past event *how* to fight. We learn from the future event *why* we fight. The *how* has to do with using the weapons of Ephesians 6: truth, justice, peace, faith, salvation, the word of God, prayer, and perseverance. The *why* has to do with making our contribution to the coming of the kingdom of God by being its agents in all areas of our lives: the individual, familial, communal, and social.

The biblical perspective knows of no split between the individual and the social (and thus goes counter to much of the ethos of modern-day North America.) All individuals are individuals-in-community. The person of faith is one with responsibility toward others, an individual full of God's love and compassion for all people. The individual does not stand alone, an isolated, lonely entity.

These "social" elements of existence do not override the individuality of the person, rather they define it and nurture it. Our ultimate "yes" or "no" to God—to following the Lamb and fighting his war his way—comes from our heart as individuals in contact with God. But we are individuals *shaped by the community* of which we are a part. We are sent out to these communities and far beyond on God's behalf.

The individual-in-community remains in a fundamental way an individual, responsible for his or her decisions and obedience to God. As obedient people of God, people of faith have the responsibility of being agents of God's peace in the world.

One part of this is to honestly face the violence within each of us—to not deny it but to confront it, to overcome it, and to redirect it in positive, creative works of service.

This "internal" peacemaking, which of course cannot happen apart from works of "external" peacemaking, can be seen as the center of a series of concentric circles. The next circle is our family and close friends, those we with whom we live in close proximity. This is followed by the circle of our church community, our neighborhood, our town or city. And finally is the circle of the wider world. This image of concentric circles is not the basis for prioritizing our peacemaking efforts but for recognizing the need to care for human life on all levels—to strive for integrity, consistency, and responsibility for living faithfully in the light of God's loving concern for all of creation.

This challenge to integrity is really part of John's overall challenge in his book to Christians—to choose the city of God over the city of Satan. The city imagery is important because it highlights the social nature of human existence. God is at work creating a new *social* reality through the community of the faithful.

But the city imagery has its drawbacks if it is used to justify withdrawal from life in the world and if we understand fleeing Babylon to mean literally separating ourselves from our non-Christian neighbors. John writes in metaphorical terms about the cities. Both take up the same space. Each exists side by side, even within each other. The citizen of the New Jerusalem, in this time before the last day, lives out that citizenship by being a faithful *witness* within Babylon.

This is a present-day challenge to us to not "hide our lights," but to actively seek to make peace however we can, wherever there is conflict. Certainly the church knows plenty of conflict. But so, too, does the wider world. We have a responsibility for the integrity of the church's witness, which certainly means that we need to deal openly with our internal problems. But if the church only focuses inwardly, then it really has no witness.

The job of identifying the shape of this witness is one which demands discernment—both of our own gifts, abilities, and interests and of the needs around us. However, the difficulty of this discernment process must not deter us from facing the implications of John's message. Once more we see the challenge in Jesus' message to the church at Laodicea: "I know your works: you are neither cold nor hot. . . . So, because you are lukewarm, and neither cold nor hot, I will spew you out of my mouth" (3:15-16). Our citizenship in God's city is determined by how we respond to the challenge to minister in Satan's city.

Jesus' own response to this challenge serves both as a demand on us and as a promise to us. His way of suffering love is the way for us to follow. It calls into question any of our shortcuts and our attempts to manipulate or disregard other people "for a greater ultimate good." His victory means that ours is also assured, should we follow in his way.

Questions for Thought and Discussion

(1) What is the significance of the bride making herself ready for the marriage supper of the Lamb? What is the role of the "the righteous deeds of the saints" (19:8)? What *are* these "righteous deeds"? How are you doing with regard to them?

(2) What do you make of the various mentions of the importance of good works (e.g., 14:13; 19:8; 20:12)? How do you relate the necessity of good works to the idea of salvation by God's grace alone?

(3) Do you see the picture in 19:11-16 as consistent with the Jesus of the Gospels? Should it be?

(4) What do you make of the apparent absence of a real battle where one is expected (19:19-20)? Assuming that this is a way of emphasizing the all-sufficiency of Jesus' cross and resurrection for defeating the forces of evil, do you think this has any relevance for present-day struggles with evil?

(5) Do you agree that the 1000 years is a symbol for the time between Christ's first and second comings? If not, how do you understand it? How important do you think this issue is? Why?

(6) What do you make of the binding of Satan (20:2)? Is it conceivable that Satan is bound now, given the rampant evil in our world?

(7) Do you believe that in the real world what seems to be defeat (i.e., persecution, even literal death, for the sake of Jesus) can really be a victory? If so, how does that belief affect your life?

(8) Is the idea of the great white throne judgment a comfort or a threat to you? Why? How is your attitude toward this related to your view of God and God's predisposition toward you?

Revelation 21 and 22

The New Jerusalem

Study Questions

   (1) What is the meaning or significance of the word "new" in 21:1? Does the remainder of the passage throw any light on its meaning?

   (2) Why is the consumation of God's purpose described in terms of a city? And why, specifically, Jerusalem?

   (3) Consider each statement of the one on the throne. How are they related to each other? What is the idea of the whole?

   (4) Note how the city in chapter 21 is portrayed. What is the meaning of the following:

> "coming down out of heaven" (21:2, 10)?
> "as a bride," "the bride" (21:2, 9)?
> the measurements of the city (21:15-16)?
> the absence of the temple (21:22)?
> the gates, the wall, and the names of each (21:12-14)?
> the gates are never closed (21:25)?
> the river . . . flowing from the throne" (22:1)?
> "the tree of life" (22:2)?

(5) What is the meaning of 21:22-23? Account for the relation of the nations to the city.

(6) Verses 6-21 of chapter 22 function as an epilogue. What important points are made here?

(7) How do you understand the statement "I am coming soon" (22:7, 12, 20)?

(8) How is the experience in 22:8-9 related to others in the book? Is this an additional one? What is its value here?

(9) Who speaks in 22:10-15? Note the ideas included in the paragraph. What is their interrelation? Explain the expectancy.

21:1-4—The New Jerusalem: Creation Transformed

God as "all in all" is what the New Jerusalem is all about. Verses 3-4 proclaim that reality: "Behold, the dwelling of God is with humankind. He will dwell with them, and they shall be his people, and God himself will be with them; he will wipe away every tear from their eyes, and death shall be no more, neither shall there be mourning nor crying nor pain any more, for the former things have passed away."

The passing away of the old order of things is pictured in 21:1 as the passing away of the first heaven, first earth, and the sea. These symbolize the ambivalence of the way things are now. Heaven is the spiritual reality, which includes both good and evil. Earth is where the church is. But it is also where the inhabitants of the earth and those who are rebellious against God are. It may also symbolize the abyss out of which the beast came.

The new heaven and earth are cleansed of the forces of evil. They are heaven and earth as purely good—the way they were created to be.

The holy city (21:2)—the beautiful bride—stands in stark contrast to Babylon. Only with a vision of the holy city can the allurements of Babylon the harlot be perceived for what they are and be resisted.

The New Jerusalem "coming down" indicates that God is *transforming*, not destroying and recreating. Note that there is something here to which it "comes down"—something already in existence which it transforms. God remains faithful to the Noahic covenant of never again destroying the earth (cf. the rainbow in 4:3).

21:5-8—*The Consummation of History*

The "newness" emphasized here is in the *consummation* of history, not a *junking* of history in order to start over with something entirely different.

This is the first time since the beginning of the visions in chapter 4 that John hears the voice of God. What God has to say, in speaking from the future, is for the present: "I am making everything new!" This activity of God is not reserved for the new creation, after the old has been discarded as garbage. Rather it is the process of *re*-creating by which the old is transformed into the new.

Verse 8 reminds us of the threat that those who choose to identify with the destroyers of the earth in their anti-God work will also identify with them in their fate of separation from God. By their own choice they will remain in Babylon.

21:9-14—*The Holy City: A Radiant Bride*

These verses are a vision of the holy city. In one sense it is future, but in another sense it exists in the present and, like Babylon, invites people to come into it. What is at stake for us now is our choice of cities.

The New Jerusalem is actually constructed of people. The people of God are the bride, which is to say that we are the walls and foundations of the city and we inhabit the city. The twelve tribes of Israel make up the walls (21:12) and the twelve apostles make up the foundation (21:14). Together they are symbolic of the whole people of God.

The city metaphorically represents a people. The earthly temple and earthly Jerusalem are destroyed. They have been replaced by the people living in the direct presence of God.

21:15-21—*The City's Measurements and Decorations*

The city is measured—like the temple in 11:1—to show that every inch of it is accounted for by God.

The city is said to be, in effect, cube-shaped: "as wide as it is long." The holy of holies in the ancient temple was a cube (1 Kings 6:20). But John insists that the city of God has no temple (21:22). This absence of the temple is something totally unparalleled in Jewish writings, which always picture the temple as being part of the future kingdom. For John, the New Jerusalem is all temple, filled with the presence of the Lord Almighty and the Lamb.

21:22-27—God's Glory Fills Everything

Everything which the temple represented the temple of old is now transferred to the life of the city. God's glory fills everything. Merely to be in the city is to be with God. God Almighty is seen in the Lamb (21:23). Jesus defines who God is. The light of the world becomes also the light by which the nations walk (21:24). They will no longer be deceived.

In John's earlier visions, the nations are deceived by Satan and are subservient to the antichrist and "the kings of the earth." But the deceiver is defeated and finally removed. Now the song of 15:4 is fulfilled: "All nations shall come and worship you."

The nations who once offered their riches to the city of the antichrist will yield them instead to the city of God and the Lamb (21:24, 26). This implies a sanctification of the whole order of the created world and its products. Nothing from the old order that has value in the sight of God is kept from entry into the new order.

Verse 27 reminds us that the city is truly holy and pure. Those who enter it do not do so because God compromises, but because they themselves have been transformed, they themselves have been made holy and pure.

22:1-5—The River and Tree of Life

In 22:2, the fruit of the tree of life symbolizes life in its fullest. The river of living water even more powerfully expresses the idea of life in inexhaustible supply. The "healing of the nations" from the "leaves of the tree of life" likely refers to healing the hurts caused by the plague judgments. The nations are healed from the awful effects of the dragon and his cohorts. This is an assertion that God is truly a God of healing who is faithful to God's promises.

The curse is no more (22:3). In Genesis 3:24, we are told that God "placed [on the east side of the Garden of Eden] the cherubim, and a flaming sword which turned every way, to guard the way to the tree of life." But in the New Jerusalem, there will no longer be a guard. The tree of life will be accessible to all who are in the city.

22:6-21—Epilogue

This section serves as an epilogue and emphasizes two themes in particular: the authenticity of the work as a revelation from God and the nearness of the fulfillment of its message.

These verses end the *letter* (cf.1:4) of which the visions are a part. John refers to his own role and authority. He echoes motifs from the first three chapters.

As early Christians understood communion, the Jesus who died and rose comes in a tangible foretaste of his final coming, which will be blessing to those who are ready; disaster to those who are not. This foretaste is powerful *now*—for good or ill. So their liturgies included sorting out the worshipers, excluding the unfit so that they might repent and become fit. This scrutiny is built into the structure of the seven letters. But in this closing section we stand beyond the scrutiny, on the brink of Jesus' final coming, when the door will be shut and knocking will be in vain (cf. Matt. 25:10). There is a last call to the hearer to choose and a final prayer to Christ to *come.*

Summary

God as "all in all" is what the New Jerusalem is all about. The new heaven and earth are cleansed of the forces of evil. They are heaven and earth as purely good, the way they were created to be. The New Jerusalem "comes down" and transforms existing creation.

The "newness" of God here should be seen as the consummation of history. God makes *all things·new,* not all new things. Redemption is the process of recreation by which the old is transformed into the new.

The New Jerusalem is actually constructed of people. The earthly temple and earthly Jerusalem are destroyed. They have been replaced by the people living in the direct presence of God. For John the New Jerusalem is *all temple,* filled with the presence of the Lord Almighty and the Lamb.

The nations who once offered their riches to the city of the anitchrist will yield them instead to the city of God and the Lamb. The healing of the nations from the leaves of the tree of life perhaps refers to healing the hurts caused by the plague judgments and the effects of the description and work of the dragon and his cohorts. The tree of life will be accessible to all who are in the city.

Meditation

From start to finish, the Bible records the fulfillment of God's purpose in creation. There has always been a longing for the time to come when true peace shall reign over all the earth. Fear, hatred, and bitter tears will be no more.

The affirmation of Revelation 21 and 22 is that this fulfillment, this conclusion of history, will be worth all the pain and struggle which humankind has experienced throughout the ages. The completion of God's work is the New Jerusalem—the establishment of the holy city—within which God's people will reign for ever and ever.

If the city of Babylon is characterized by terror, deception, and injustice, the New Jerusalem is the exact opposite. There the nations walk in harmony and justice and peace, where the light of the glory of God guides everyone's path.

Reflecting on this vision of John's is encouraging in two ways. First, it strongly affirms the powers of evil are not ultimate. God will have the final word. The book of Revelation is unsparing in its portrayal of how strong and powerful evil is in the world. What we have, of course, is a picture—a vision—not a rational, detailed description. It is painted with bold and lurid colors and does not correspond in every detail to reality as it is discerned by human eyes.

It is obvious enough to us, however, that the beast, the dragon, the harlot, and their cohorts greatly affect human existence. Widespread suffering and destruction has been caused by military violence throughout human history. But war is just one concern among many. It is easy for me to despair and to believe that things are getting worse and will inevitably keep getting worse.

However, Revelation 21 and the vision of the New Jerusalem claim that this evil will not last forever. God is not powerless to stop it. The powers of love and compassion and forgiveness will win. This means that the coming of God's city is a realistic goal. The hope that this city is coming is a hope worth living (and dying for)—worth shaping one's life by.

The second reason for encouragement has to do with the emphasis in this vision on the *renewing* of creation. God is "making all things new," not "making all new things." We can thus affirm and appreciate God's creation in a fresh way. We can love the beauty and mysteries of nature. We can appreciate all the cultural and scientific accomplishments humankind has achieved that genuinely make life better. We can appreciate and create art of all kinds.

We do not have to feel alienated from these good things as if they are part of the old order which is passing away. That the harpers, minstrels, flute players, and trumpeters will not be heard in Babylon after it is destroyed, and that the craftsmen will not be found there anymore does not mean that there will not be music and crafts. There still will be art and creativity in the New Jerusalem; the splendor of the nations will be brought to the city (21:26).

Creation was intended to contribute to human fulfillment. Tragically, it is often misused. When creation itself is worshiped, rather than the Creator, it becomes an instrument of oppression and bondage. The harlot, Babylon, is destroyed so that this deception might end and so that legitimate human accomplishments may be enjoyed.

The task for us as Christians in this "millennium" before the fullness of the New Jerusalem is to live as free as possible from the deception. This deception causes us to want to replace God as the center of our lives with products of human culture, such as art, money, crafts, or our profession. When we are free from that kind of deception, we are free to enjoy and produce works of human creativity as part of our worship of God.

Just as the "city" of Babylon in chapters 17 and 18 is not a literal city but rather symbolic of the concentrated forces of evil, the New Jerusalem is also not meant to be a literal city. Babylon is the kingdom of the dragon; Jerusalem in this vision is the kingdom of God.

The kingdom of God—the New Jerusalem—is made up of *people*. A key element in John's vision is that the New Jerusalem, in all its brilliance and beauty, is not something people visit or take residence in. Rather, it is something people *become*. The people of God are often referred to in the New Testament as the bride of Christ. Here, in 21:9-11, we are told that John "saw the bride, the wife of the Lamb," which was the holy city, Jerusalem, coming down out of heaven from God, possessing the glory of God.

In Paul's terminology (see Romans 8:19), the "revealing of the children of God" takes place with the coming of the New Jerusalem.

The New Jerusalem is where God dwells directly with his people. It is where all who have all been made new and who see God's face and reign for ever and ever with the Lamb.

The hope for all creation, as Paul describes it in Romans 8 is this revealing of the children of God as the New Jerusalem: "Creation will be set free from its bondage to decay." No more will the creation be exploited and polluted by greedy humankind.

God makes all things new. The coming of the New Jerusalem means that all of creation will be renewed—that the redeemed people who make up the city will have with them all that is truly good and beautiful in this world. So the New Jerusalem, the city of God, is made up of people—the countless multitudes that John sees singing praises to the Lamb throughout the book. But along with these renewed people will be all of creation—purified and set free from the bondage of decay and death. It will not be worshiped instead of God, but cared for and enjoyed as part of *God's* creation.

In Revelation 22:2 John sees a river flowing through the middle of the city on either side of which is "the tree of life with its twelve kinds of fruit, yielding its fruit each month; and the leaves of the tree were for the healing of the nations." This healing of the nations is consistent with the renewal of creation and human culture. It furthermore implies the healing of the hurt caused by the work of God in destroying evil in human history.

Many people and many parts of creation are damaged by evil and greatly in need of healing. The message of this vision is that *healing will happen.* Wholeness is promised to the nations and the creation.

What are the implications of this vision of John's for us today? One implication comes from the side-by-side placing of Babylon and Jerusalem. The big issue in this time between Jesus' life, death, and resurrection and the final revealing of the New Jerusalem is *the loyalty of people.* Are we part of Babylon or are we part of Jerusalem? The values and spiritual realities symbolized by these two cities stand together on earth. Each invites people to come and enjoy its blessings.

To John it is clear which city offers life and which offers death. To us, it is not always so clear. But we are constantly faced with the choice: Do we follow the way of the Lamb or not? The little choices we make now determine what kind of people we become and in which city we will be at home.

John's vision is a vision of hope, of promise. The New Jerusalem will come down, heaven and earth will be one, and God will dwell with God's people. This is meant to be an encouragement to John's readers in their times of tribulation, persecution, and temptation. These things will not last. They will not have the final say. So be of good cheer. Hold strongly to what is true. Remain faithful to the way of the Lamb, the way of love. Do so because this is the way of God, the Creator of the universe and the Redeemer of his creation.

This is not just a vision of some far-off future about which we do not have to be concerned now. Rather, it is God's perspective on the present reality. It is God's current agenda. It will be completed in the future, but we are called to be a part of the process. We are called to identify with the Lamb now and walk in his ways, to have our lives shaped by the kind of sacrificial love and forgiveness that shaped Jesus' life.

Questions for Thought and Discussion

(1) What do you tend to associate with the New Jerusalem? Do you see it as totally future? or in some sense present? Or is it a pie-in-the-sky-by-and-by (i.e., a means of avoiding the present-day reality)?

(2) How does hope of the New Jerusalem impinge on your present, if at all? Can this hope help or even push one to suffer for justice in the present? Or does it more likely allow one to deny responsibility for such action?

(3) Does the promise that there will be no more mourning and crying help one to embrace mourning and crying in the present?

(4) Do you agree that the New Jerusalem "coming down" (21:2) indicates a transforming of things and not a destruction and recreation? Is this distinction important?

(5) How much continuity is there between human history and the New Jerusalem? How much, if any, of our work will be included there?

(6) What do you make of the assertion in 21:24 that "the kings of the earth" are inside God's new city? How could this be? Is it something you would welcome? Why or why not?

(7) Do you see any evidence in your own experience (and what

you know of history) that God is in the process of transforming the fallen world into the New Jerusalem? If so, what evidence do you have? Is there any evidence that evil is not ultimate and all-powerful?

(8) Do you agree that the "healing of the nations" from the "leaves of the tree" of life (22:2) refers to healing the hurts caused by the plague judgments and the effects of the work of the dragon and his cohorts? Does this image make the plague visions seem less total, absolute, ultimate?

(9) How do you understand "Behold, I am coming soon" (22:7, 10)? Is 2000 years "soon"? Do you expect him to come "soon"? How soon is soon?

Conclusion

The Meaning of Revelation for Today

Study Questions

If possible, reread the whole book in one sitting. Even better, listen to it being read aloud.

(1) Does the book make sense to you now?

(2) What are the key themes?

(3) How does Revelation speak to you?

(4) How does Revelation relate to the church in the modern world?

(5) What are your biggest unanswered questions?

(6) What in this study guide has struck you in a new and helpful way? What have you found with which you cannot agree?

(7) Do you feel hopeful, unhopeful, or hopelessly confused in rereading Revelation? Why?

Questions for Thought and Discussion
(with some attempted answers)

(1) Why has Jesus not yet returned? Why does history go on?

This is not a big issue if we remember that one day equals 1000 years in God's sight. What seems like a long time to us does not necessarily seem so to God.

Yet history does continue. Why keep it going at all? One could say that God does not want anyone to perish, so God keeps history going in order to give them a chance. But people keep being born and the net effect would appear to be more negative than positive.

What is at stake in this in-between time prior to Jesus' second coming is people's loyalty. History goes on in order to test that loyalty.

Revelation suggests that history continues so that God's purposes will be fulfilled. These purposes cannot be fulfilled otherwise. We cannot understand all the reasons for this. They are tied to the mysteries of evil and of human free will. These purposes entail the ultimate self-destruction of evil. History continues so that evil can run its course and in the end be totally destroyed.

The affirmation of Revelation, if we can believe it, is that God is in control of history and that God is working things out in God's own way. There are glimpses of the idea that Jesus cannot come back before evil runs its course. Otherwise, God would be stifling human free will and would actually become an agent of coercion and ultimately of evil.

(2) What is the purpose of God's judgment? Is it primarily to condemn God's enemies? or to purify God's friends?

My views of God are based on more than the book of Revelation. I believe that God loves God's enemies and is always seeking to make them friends by offering them forgiveness and the transforming power of God's Spirit.

The threats of judgment, sometimes communicated as promises of judgment but always conditional, are part of this process. God threatens judgment in order for people to turn back to God. The judgment itself is intended to be purifying. In effect, God wants to weed out the "tares" from our "wheat." If we do not have any wheat, there will be nothing left when the tares are gone. The practical result, then, is condemnation. But it is self-condemnation. In our rejection of God we may experience God's purifying "weeding" as a destructive thing—even though God's intention is purification and not condemnation.

God's real enemies, whom God does not love, are the spiritual forces of evil: the dragon, the beast, the false prophet, and the harlot.

God must destroy them so that God's human "enemies"—whom God loves—can possibly escape destruction. The ultimate purpose of the visions of judgment is to show that God is working to destroy these forces and that—hard as it may be to believe it—God will complete this work. Christians are thus exhorted to cultivate their wheat so that when Babylon falls they are not caught in its collapse.

(3) How is evil conquered? What role do Christians have to play?

Evil is conquered by a nonretaliatory love that refuses to get caught up in the cycle of evil begetting evil. Rather this love lets God's wrath take its course. The ultimate effect of God's wrath is the self-destruction of evil. The central and decisive act of love in this process was Jesus' death. Jesus did not fight back, but rather trusted totally in God's power. The forces of evil battered Jesus, but his resurrection in God's power insured their destruction. In Revelation, evil is never resisted in kind, but only by the power of a love that does not bow the knee.

Christians play no role in the decisive defeat of evil. That was done by Jesus on their behalf. For all its battle imagery, Revelation communicates clearly that the real battle is past history.

Nonetheless, a secondary battle rages on, limited to earth. It does not take place in the ultimate reality of heaven. This battle is important, because the fate of human beings is decided by which side they are on—the winning side or the losing side.

The way to remain on the winning side, and the way to influence others to join that side, is to "follow the Lamb wherever he goes." In other words, the responsibility of Christians in the battle with evil is to always remain faithful to Jesus' way of nonretaliatory love—even in the face of calls to take up arms against godless communism and other threats. In the struggle against evil, a good end never justifies an evil means. The true end is achieved by God alone and never by human attempts to take things into one's hands and achieve by coercion and violence what God achieves only by love.

(4) Are the values of antichrist present in our world today? If so, what might they be? How are we tempted to assimilate and accept them?

The values of the antichrist are especially insidious and include the desire for power. Instead of trusting wholly on God for one's security, the spirit of antichrist will attempt to provide self-security. Instead of looking to God for direction in life, the spirit of antichrist will look elsewhere for direction and for decision-making criteria. In contrast, Christ's values center around the will to serve and around total trust in God.

In this broad understanding, the values of antichrist have existed ever since Adam and Eve. And they will continue to exist until the final judgment. Our crucial temptations are generally in day-to-day kinds of things.

Decisions about these things determine what kind of people we really are becoming. And what kind of people we really are is what determines how we make the more crucial decisions if and when the need arises.

Those who are motivated by the will to power misplace their trust and seek security outside of God. They learn different values. If we reach that point, then our battle with antichrist is lost regardless of how literally Revelation's visions are fulfilled or how religious our veneer.

The pastoral concern of John is that day by day—the "little" things—we follow the Lamb wherever he goes. We can miss this if we think of the prophecies of Revelation as primarily predicting future, events which we do not have to worry about right now.

(5) Is there anything in the teaching of Revelation that might encourage us to try to make the world better?

The tone of Revelation seems to imply that this world is hopelessly evil and is passing away. Our main concern should be one of holding fast and not joining with that evil—remaining strong of heart even when persecuted. Not much is made, it would appear, of trying to make the world better.

To a large degree this characterization is accurate. To some extent it reflects the simple reality of the church's situation. That was what they needed to hear. The possibility of transforming their culture was simply unthinkable at that time.

Our question is, Is this a statement for all times and places? Is this the simple reality for all Christians and to think otherwise is to compromise with the beast?

I am not sure. I believe Christians should try to make the world better. Elements in Revelation support this belief:

(a) The readers are repeatedly exhorted to do good works. Even evangelism narrowly defined can be seen as an attempt to make the world better.

(b) The picture of the New Jerusalem shows the kings of the earth bringing their splendor into it (21:24) and the nations bringing their glory and honor into it (21:26). Thus, the good that is accomplished now is carried into the New Jerusalem. In other words, what we do—what we accomplish—really matters.

(c) The transition from the old age into the new age is more gradual than the apocalyptic imagery in Revelation might suggest. The stark and explosive imagery appears more for its dramatic effect than for predicting what will happen. So our faithfulness may help to bring about the kingdom as part of the leavening process.

(6) Are the plagues pictured in Revelation inevitable? Is there nothing we can do to stop them? Or are they pictures of what *might* happen, implying that we should work to keep them from happening?

To a large degree, the plagues are pictures of what *has* happened, *is* happening, and *will continue* to happen as long as evil exists. They have to happen in order for evil to be destroyed, but they will cease when there is no need for them.

Evil's only power is deception. When we see it for what it is and reject it, its power in effect ceases to exist. Less evil means fewer plagues. Our goal should be to facilitate the coming of the kingdom. When the kingdom comes, the plagues will cease. New plagues will not appear.

The plagues are not absolutely inevitable because evil is not absolutely inevitable. We should work and pray that the plagues might not come, believing that they need not come and that one day they will be over—once and for all.

Our faithfulness does not depend on our success in stopping the plagues. But we should with our whole being try to stop them, trusting in God's promise that God will reward us for doing so by transforming us into people who are totally at home in a place without plagues, where every tear is wiped away (21:4).

(7) Does Revelation tell us anything that provides meaning to human suffering?

The author and the immediate recipients of this book were facing suffering in the present—with the anticipation of more to come. The meaning of suffering is thus a central one in this book.

John, however, is not concerned with suffering as such. Rather, he is concerned about a specific kind of suffering—suffering that is chosen, suffering that people take on themselves as a result of their choice to faithfully witness to Jesus. The churches at Laodicea and Sardis were doing fine without suffering. Suffering for them was not inevitable. But they were also being unfaithful. They were not really following Jesus.

For those who would follow Jesus, suffering is likely. The readers of Revelation risked social ostracism and persecution if they did not take part in the pagan festivals and emperor worship. If they stood for justice in an unjust society, the powers that be would see them as a threat and seek to remove that threat.

This suffering had meaning because it meant people were following the way Jesus took in conquering evil. To suffer because of faithfulness is to be part of God's work in bringing in the kingdom. The only hope for the world is that Jesus and his followers stand free from the power of evil. But doing so almost always entails suffering.

Revelation also seems to imply that arbitrary kinds of suffering are not really arbitrary. Satan is at work in the world trying his best to mar God's creation and to turn people against God. All suffering is therefore a test. Will we turn to God as our only Lord or will we follow the advice of Job's wife and "curse God, and die" (Job 2:9)?

(8) How does Jesus rule? To what does the "iron scepter" (2:27; 12:5; 19:15) refer?

Revelation does not say much about how Jesus rules. It presents the paradoxical picture of a conquering Lamb. But the Gospels say a lot about his style of leadership: servanthood. The imagery of conquering symbolizes his decisive spiritual victory over evil through the power of love.

The Jesus of the Gospels and the Lamb are one and the same. Jesus does not change his character between his first and second comings. The crucial and decisive battle happened at the cross, not

Armageddon. If the way of love was the way *that* battle was won, it would seem silly to think that any later, secondary battle might be won differently.

The Lamb concept should determine our understanding of things like the iron scepter—not vice versa. The iron scepter symbol comes from Psalm 2 and is obviously a reference to the Messiah's rule. It is a statement of the Messiah's sovereign rule. But the actual character of that sovereignty—when the Messiah Jesus did come— turned out to be much different than that of the warrior king envisioned in Psalm 2.

Many first-century Jews missed their Messiah because they misunderstood the character of his rule. It seems that many twentieth-century Christians are repeating the same mistake. Many still think Jesus will return as a literal warrior king. This Christological mistake is then made an ethical mistake when they shape their present-day values around that concept (e.g., in support of militarism and capital punishment).

(9) How can we be "sealed" by God (7:1-3)? From what does this protect us?

Being "sealed" by God and having God's name written on one's forehead (14:1) are both picturesque ways of expressing identification with God—being filled with God's Spirit.

What is at stake in the world between Christ's comings is people's loyalties. People must choose between living in the harlot's city—Babylon—or the bride's city, the New Jerusalem. Those who choose the New Jerusalem will be challenged in that choice. They will be threatened with suffering—even death—by the dragon and his cohorts.

John's point in speaking of "sealing" is to emphasize that the dragon cannot separate people of faith from God's love. John refers to the first death and the second death. The former is physical death and the latter is final separation from God at the judgment day. Those who are "sealed" by God are guaranteed protection from the second death, even if they prematurely go through the first death.

Those that trust in God are promised that God will neither leave them nor forsake them (Ps. 37:28). That is what the sealing indicates. As long as people trust in God, God will stay with them and bring them through death to resurrection. Because of this, John can call upon God's people to hold on to their faith.

(10) How can one reconcile in Revelation the appearance of both mass punishment (chapters 6; 8-9; 16) and mass salvation (5:9ff.; 7:9ff.; 21:24ff.)?

The idea of "prophetic paradox" may help us here. A number of the Old Testament prophets used this method. God will save the people and God will destroy the people. At times it seems almost as if both are stated in the same breath.

The purpose of the prophet was not to provide information for its own sake. The purpose was to move people to repentance and obedience. The prophets did not always concern themselves with inner consistency and clear logic. When saying, "this *will* happen," they might actually mean "this will happen *unless. . . .*"

The positive promises of the prophets (including John in Revelation) of mass salvation are statements of faith. They believed that God would bring about the New Jerusalem and that countless people would be part of it.

The negative statements about mass punishment are not promises of what will happen to those outside of our community. The book of Revelation was written to the community of faith—not to unbelievers. Its warnings are therefore warnings to *us*: This is where *we* might end up if we continue on our rebellious path. The Bible is not given to speculation about the fate of those outside the community of faith. Its concern is to call those within that community to faithfulness.

Mass punishment is used in Revelation as a technique—to exhort people in the church to examine themselves. It was not meant as a factual statement about those outside the church.

Perhaps John was using a carrot-and-stick approach: You should be faithful so you can be part of the singing multitude and not part of the cursing multitude.

(11) What is the significance of the numerous mentions of good works (2:2; 2:19; 3:1; 3:8; 3:15; 14:13; 19:8; 20:12)? How does this relate to Paul's teaching of justification by faith alone?

Both Paul and John integrally connected faith and works. Entry into the book of life is not based on our relative merit, but on our acceptance of God's grace by faith. But if we do not obey Christ—if we do not do good works—we have no basis for claiming to be in the book of life. We cannot know God's grace apart from knowing it as a power that motivates and empowers us to do good works.

John implies in his vision of the white throne judgment in 20:11-15 that a person cannot truly do good works without faith. (This is also implied in Jesus' teaching and to some degree in Paul's.) So if a person is judged to have done good works, it can be assumed that he or she had faith—even if that faith was not clearly articulated in totally orthodox terms. Conversely, if a person espouses the best doctrines but is not judged to have done good works, it can be assumed that that person did not really have true faith.

The letters to the churches show John's pastoral concerns. The rest of the book addresses those concerns. The churches are exhorted very strongly regarding the importance of their works. It follows, therefore, that the rest of the book was intended to lead its readers to good works, not to idle speculation about the meaning of 666, the location of Armageddon, or the specific person who is or will be the antichrist.

(12) How can it be that Satan, the beast and their cohorts are so powerful and yet, in the end are so easily defeated?

Satan is so easily defeated in the end because his real defeat came when Christ was crucified and rose from the dead (i.e., when the Lamb was found worthy to take the scroll in chapter 5). Therefore, all Christ has to do in 19:20 and 20:10 is capture the dragon, beast, and false prophet and throw them into the lake of fire. The real battle is long past by that time.

How, if he was defeated so decisively on the cross, could the devil and his cohorts appear to be so powerful? God apparently allows Satan to exert power even after that decisive defeat. But Satan has no power that God does not allow him to exercise and can do nothing that will not ultimately serve God's purposes.

Revelation has no answer for why God would want to do this. Somehow, for God to eradicate evil totally, Satan needs to continue to operate for a while longer. Evil exists outside of us—as a force personified as the devil—but it also exists in the human heart.

The evil outside of us exploits the evil inside, but to God it is of much less consequence. God can end it with a flick of the wrist. God is after the evil inside. God wants to destroy *it* without destroying *us*. Somehow, in a way we cannot fully understand, to ultimately take care of the evil inside the human heart, God must allow Satan some time to operate. John's final word, however, is that Satan's time is short. We may not always see it, but God is doing away with evil and the New Jerusalem is coming.

Bibliography

Bible Study Guides

Barclay, William. *The Revelation of John*, 2 volumes. Philadelphia: Westminster, 1960. 231 and 297 pp. Part of Barclay's New Testament commentary series. Special emphasis on devotionally oriented word studies. Good on historical background. Strongly preterist, though he draws spiritual applications for today.

Perkins, Pheme. *The Book of Revelation*. Collegeville, Minn.: Liturgical Press, 1983. 93 pp. Quite brief but often insightful study by a prominent New Testament scholar with some study aids.

Schüssler Fiorenza, Elisabeth. *The Apocalypse*. Chicago: Franciscan Herald, 1976. 62 pp. A short study for lay people by preeminent Revelation scholar writing today.

_____. *Invitation to the Book of Revelation*. Garden City, NY: Doubleday, 1981. 223 pp. An excellent resource for the serious student. Includes helpful allusions to social concerns.

Yarbro Collins, Adela. *Apocalypse*. Wilmington, Del., Michael Glazier, 1980. 155 pp. A quite solid study guide for laypersons by an authoritative scholar.

Commentaries

Beasley-Murray, George. *The Book of Revelation*. Grand Rapids, Mich., Eerdmans, 1974. 352 pp. One of the best modern semi-scholarly commentaries. Mildly futurist. Sees much relevance for present-day Christian life. Helpful emphasis on theology.

Beckwith, Ibsen T. *The Apocalypse of John*. Grand Rapids, Mich., Baker, 1922. 794 pp. Probably the best full-scale commentary. Though now old, still of considerable value. Over 400 pages of introduction. Primarily preterist.

Caird, George B. *A Commentary on the Revelation of St. John the Divine*. New York: Harper and Row, 1966. 316 pp. My favorite commentary. Mainly combines pretarist with symbolic viewpoints. Strong emphasis on ethical implications. Sees martyrdom as a central motif and treads lightly on the punitive force of God's judgment. Well-written.

Eller, Vernard, *The Most Revealing Book in the Bible*. Grand Rapids, Mich. Eerdmans, 1974. 214 pp. A popular-level study featuring Eller's unique cleverness. A quite provocative approach arguing in favor of pacifism and universalism.

Mounce, Robert T. *The Book of Revelation*. Grand Rapids, Mich., Eerdmans, 1977. 426 pp. Excellent for surveying the spectrum of interpretive opinion on many passages. Mounce himself is quite conservative and futuristic, though he rejects dispensationalism.

Smith, J. B., *A Revelation of Jesus Christ*. Scottdale, Pa.: Herald, 1961. 369 pp. A futuristically oriented commentary in the dispensational tradition by a Mennonite New Testament scholar.

Sweet, J. P. M. *Revelation*. Philadelphia: Westminster, 1979. 361 pp. A commentary similar to Caird's in viewpoint—generally quite good.

Walvoord, John. *The Revelation of Jesus Christ*. Chicago: Moody, 1966. 350 pp. The standard recent serious dispensational commentary which essentially argues for the perspective popularized by Hal Lindsey.

NOTE: Two important commentaries are expected to be published soon. Elisabeth Schüssler Fiorenza is writing what promises to be *the* detailed scholarly commentary for the Hermeneia series (published by Fortress

Press). David Aune, whose important study on New Testament prophecy is listed below, is writing the commentary for the Word Biblical Commentary series (published by Word Books).

Studies

Barclay, William. *Letters to the Seven Churches.* Nashville: Abingdon, 1957. 111 pp. A well-written, popular-level collection of studies. Especially helpful in giving background and word studies.

Ellul, Jacques. *Apocalypse: The Book of Revelation.* New York: Seabury, 1977. 283 pp. The prominent French social critic writes in a difficult style, but his insights are often profound and always stimulating.

Ramsay, William. *The Letters to the Seven Churches of Asia.* Grand Rapids: Baker, 1904. 446 pp. A study—still unsurpassed—utilizing archaeological data; on the background and meaning of the letters.

Rissi, *Time and History.* Atlanta: John Knox, 1966. 147 pp. An important, tightly reasoned, scholarly treatment of the message of Revelation. Believes Revelation meant to give a philosophy of history pointing toward total reconciliation of all things in Jesus Christ.

Shüssler Fiorenza, Elisabeth. *The Book of Revelation: Justice and Judgment,* Philadelphia: Fortress, 1985. xxi + 211 pp. A collection of insightful, though fairly technical, studies on Revelation.

Yarbro Collins, Adela. *Crisis and Catharsis: The Power of the Apocalypse.* Philadelphia: Westminster, 1984. 169 pp. A quite useful study of the background and message of Revelation, not entirely sympathetic with John's efforts.

Background

Aune, David. *Prophecy in Early Christianity and the Ancient Mediterranean World.* Grand Rapids, Mich.: Eerdmans, 1983. xii + 522 pp. A wide-ranging scholarly study. Provides invaluable material for understanding the context of John's ministry.

Collins, John J. *The Apocalyptic Imagination: An Introduction to the Jewish Matrix of Christianity.* New York: Crossroad, 1984. viii + 280 pp. A scholarly introduction to the apocalyptic tradition.

Hanson, Paul D.*The Dawn of Apocalyptic.* Philadelphia: Fortress, 1975. 426 pp. An important of the Old Testament origins of the apocalyptic tradition in the Hebrew prophets.

Minear, Paul S. *New Testament Apocalyptic.* Nashville: Abingdon, 1981. 157 pp. An interesting introduction to the use of apocalyptic in the New Testament with concern for present-day application.

NOTE: New Testament introductions are often helpful sources for background information. Unfortunately most popular-level introductions pay little attention to Revelation. The standard scholarly ones include:

Brevard Childs. *The New Testament as Canon: An Introduction.* Philadelphia: Fortress, 1985.

Donald Guthrie. *New Testament Introduction.* Downers Grove, Ill.: Inter-Varsity, 1970.

Helmut Koester. *Introduction to the New Testament*, vol. 2. Philadelphia: Fortress, 1982.

Werner Georg Kümmel, *Introduction to the New Testament.* Nashville: Abingdon, 1975.

Ralph P. Martin. *New Testament Foundations*, vol. 2. Grand Rapids: Eerdmans, 1978.

Perhaps even more helpful are the articles in the *Interpreter's Dictionary of the Bible*, George Buttrick, ed., Nashville: Abingdon, 1962, and supplementary volume, Keith Crim, ed., 1976; and the *International Standard Bible Encyclopedia*, revised edition, Geoffrey Bromiley, ed., Grand Rapids, Mich.: Eerdmans, 1979- . Especially helpful are those on the book of Revelation and apocalyptic literature.

Index of Scriptures

and Other Ancient Writings

Other
Ancient
Writings

The Author

Ted Grimsrud was born in Eugene, Oregon. He is a graduate of Elkton (Oreg.) High School and the University of Oregon, where he received a B.S. in Journalism. He also received a Master of Arts in Peace Studies from the Goshen Biblical Seminary in Elkhart, Indiana.

Grimsrud joined the Mennonite Church in 1981, attracted by Mennonite concerns for discipleship, peacemaking, and community. He has served as coordinator of Christians for Peace and Justice, a peace advocacy ministry sponsored by the Eugene (Oreg.) Mennonite Church. He also served as an interim pastor with the Eugene Mennonite Church and Trinity Mennonite Church in Glendale, Arizona.

Currently he is a Ph.D. candidate in Religion and Society at the Graduate Theological Union in Berkeley, California. His area of concentration is Christian ethics. He attends the First Mennonite Church of San Francisco.

Grimsrud lives in Berkeley, California, with his wife, Kathy Temple, and son Johan.